A Goushā Weekend Guide

California Bike Tours

64 detailed bike routes, each with its own map showing all
traveled roads and key intersections

GOUSHĀ
TIMES MIRROR

GOUSHĀ PUBLICATIONS
San Jose, California

Edited by Marian May
Cover design by Roger Waterman
Cover illustration by Masami Miyamoto

We thank Paul Schwemler, President of the League
of American Wheelmen, Dr. Clifford Graves, Paul
DeWitt and Ed Steffani for the selection of tours;
and the many cycling clubs and bicycle shops for
assistance in the preparation of this book.
Our thanks, also, to Steve Webber for photos.

ISBN No. 0-913040-16-9
Library of Congress No. 72-80662
Printed in the United States
First edition 1972
First printing July 1972

Table of Contents

How To Use "California Bike Tours"

Whether young or old, strong or weak, big or small, everybody wants to discover new worlds.

The world of the bicycle is one of fresh air and soft breezes, clear views and sharp responses, deep breaths and quickened pulse, keen appetite and sound sleep. A world of far horizons and sweet freedom, of physical zest and mental rest. In short, a world of rich and immediate rewards. And it isn't hard to find.

To play tennis, you must have a tennis court. For golf you have to have a golf course. To go sailing, you must have a lake. For fishing, a stream; and for skiing, you must have snow. To go surfing, you have to have an ocean. But to go bicycling, you need only a bicycle—and a road.

There are hundreds of California streets and roads where you can ride a bicycle. But not everybody knows where to find them. Ideally, a cyclist needs roads with a good surface, little traffic, and varied scenery. These were the criteria used in the compilation of this book. It shows California roads that have been found especially suitable by the cyclists who live in the area. However, since this book was prepared, road and highway situations may have changed. If you are in doubt, ask directions locally.

Of course, California is hilly. If you were to cut out the hills, you would cut out the best rides. The solution lies in the other direction: learn how to cope with hills. The ten-speed bicycle allows you to do this. It allows you to gear down until you can climb the grade in the same cadence as you ride on the flat. Bicycling is a skill, to be learned just like tennis, golf, swimming and all other sports. Many people are satisfied merely to stay upright when they ride a bicycle. It's like people who use a typewriter all their lives and never progress beyond the hunt-and-peck stage. A skillful cyclist stands out because he rides straight and pedals rapidly, that is, at a rapid cadence. He maintains that cadence in the hills by gearing down. The secret is to shift gears an instant *before* you need them.

When you first begin your explorations by bicycle, you will be surprised how much more you see than you ever did before. Instead of a blur, the road becomes a sharply defined object. A house, a tree, a flower—they all vie for attention. On a bicycle, you get very close to all these things. You become more aware, and in becoming more aware, you become a more discriminating person.

Cycling is good not only for the body but for the mind. It is the most relaxing form of exercise known to man with the possible exception of walking.

The trips described in this book are of varying difficulty. In each area there are easy tours, those of moderate difficulty and others that are real rides for experienced cyclists, including a week-long, San Francisco to Los Angeles ride.

A tours are the most difficult, usually 50 miles or more with severe grades.

B tours are about 30 to 40 miles with moderate grades.

C tours are 30 miles, more or less, without steep hills.

You will see that even for a "C" ride, you have to have some experience. However, the average person should quickly learn. Beyond the "C" level, progress depends much on how much cycling you are able to do. The maps will guide you over tested routes, indicating highways and nearby points of interest. In all tours follow the direction of the starting arrows, showing the best ways to avoid headwinds, steep uphill climbs, and other negatives of bicycling.

The quickest way to become a skillful cyclist is to join a club. You learn proper style and equipment just by watching the others. If you do not know of a club in your area, write to the League of American Wheelmen, 5540 South Westmont, Whittier 90601.

And now, go to it. Happy cycling!

Dr. Clifford L. Graves, Surgeon
La Jolla, California

Los Angeles Area

(Selected by Paul Schwemler)

Palos Verdes Oceanfront Loop

Approx. mileage: 24

Rating: B

Terrain: Mostly flat, with some hills at the northern end of the loop.

Best times for touring: Good all year. Big problem here is traffic, especially on weekends. Palos Verdes Drive is very heavily traveled, and cyclists have to be attentive to traffic conditions. Not recommended for beginners or those unfamiliar with riding on congested roads.

This highly scenic route takes you through the beautiful Palos Verdes area and past some of the top tourist attractions in Los Angeles. Palos Verdes Plaza is a well-known landmark and the ideal place to start the loop; it is located at the intersection of Palos Verdes Drive North and Palos Verdes Drive West.

From the Plaza, it's best to take the ocean leg of the loop first. The views along here are spectacular, and a slow ride through Palos Verdes Estates adds to the enjoyment.

Point Vicente Lighthouse is an especially pretty landmark. Unfortunately, you can look inside only a few hours a week—Tuesdays and Thursdays from 2 to 4 p.m.

If you can spare the time, Marineland of the Pacific is always a rewarding stop. It is open daily from 10 a.m. to sunset, and no matter what time you arrive, there's bound to be some kind of show going on in one of the tanks.

The striking Wayfarer's Chapel is another good stopping point. It is situated atop a scenic bluff, and is open daily to visitors.

South of Portugese Bend, the route drops down into San Pedro. If you're looking for a rest point, Royal Palms Beach Park has some fine tidepools for exploring and the northern half of the park has picnic tables and stone fireplaces under towering palms.

Point Fermin Park is a favorite lunch stop for cyclists who favor this loop. A restaurant provides necessary nourishment while you sit and enjoy the views of ocean and historic lighthouse.

Cabrillo Beach State Park is fine for picnicking and sunning. If the tide is right, you can also spend some time looking at odd creatures in the tidepools. The park's marine museum is open daily, and tours of the marine life refuge are conducted on weekends and holidays.

After lunch, head straight for Ports O'Call Village and Whaler's Wharf, where you can spend hours browsing through the many shops, buying small imported goods and even tasting some wines.

For the last leg on the trip, you'll cycle along Western Avenue, then head back to the Plaza along beautiful Palos Verdes Drive North.

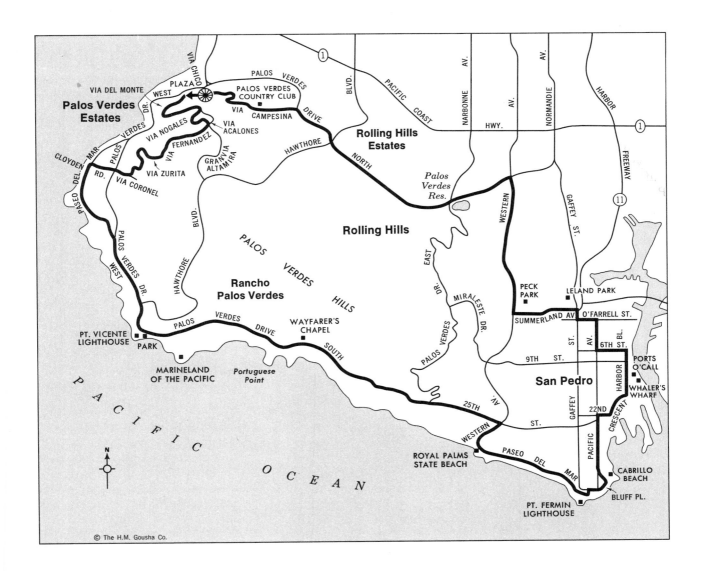

PALOS VERDES
COUNTRY CLUB

Palos Verdes Estates

VIA DEL MONTE
PLAZA
WEST
PALOS VERDES DR.
VIA NOGALES
VIA FERNANDEZ
VIA ACALONES
VIA CAMPESINA
PALOS VERDES DRIVE
VIA ZURITA
VIA CORONEL
GRAN VIA ALTAMIRA
HAWTHORE

CLOYDEN
PASEO DEL MAR
RD.

PALOS VERDES WEST DR.

HAWTHORE BLVD.

Rolling Hills Estates

Rolling Hills

Palos Verdes Res.

PALOS VERDES HILLS

Rancho
Palos Verdes

WAYFARER'S
CHAPEL

EAST PALOS VERDES DR.

MIRALESTE DR.

PALOS VERDES

WESTERN

PECK PARK

LELAND PARK

SUMMERLAND AV.
O'FARRELL ST.

San Pedro

9TH ST.
GAFFEY ST.
6TH ST.
HARBOR BL.

PORTS O'CALL
WHALER'S WHARF

22ND
CRESCENT

PACIFIC

25TH AV.

WESTERN ST.

PASEO DEL MAR

ROYAL PALMS
STATE BEACH

CABRILLO BEACH

BLUFF PL.

PT. FERMIN
LIGHTHOUSE

PT. VICENTE
LIGHTHOUSE
PARK

MARINELAND
OF THE PACIFIC

Portuguese
Point

PALOS VERDES DRIVE SOUTH

PACIFIC OCEAN

N

NARBONNE AV.
NORMANDIE AV.
HARBOR FREEWAY

PACIFIC COAST HWY.

1

11

© The H.M. Gousha Co.

9

Art, Gardens and UCLA

Approx. mileage: 12

Rating: C

Terrain: Good roads with moderate hills.

Best times for touring: Good all year round. Biking is better on the weekends when the traffic is light.

This route takes you to the Los Angeles campus of the University of California. The campus is filled with bicycle trails which lead to many interesting sights.

Starting from La Cienega Park, ride west down Olympic Boulevard to Westwood Avenue, then turn right toward UCLA. Just after passing Santa Monica Boulevard, you will see a huge white structure on a hill to the right. This is the Mormon Temple, largest of all the temples of the Mormon faith, standing 257 feet in height. On top of the spire is a 15-foot gold leaf statue of the Angel Moroni, visible 25 miles out at sea.

The temple itself is not open to the public, but you may tour the beautiful grounds. Movies of the interior of the temple are shown in the Visitor Information Center from 7 a.m. to 5 p.m. daily.

Turn left on Le Conte to begin the UCLA loop. You can ride the perimeter of the campus via Gayley, Veteran, Sunset Boulevard and Hilgard. Or you can pick any one of the many side streets that lead into the campus with its enjoyable network of bike paths. You can spend hours riding through the lovely grounds and surveying the college structures.

One of the most interesting buildings on campus is the Dickson Art Center. Inside are several galleries for travelling exhibits, and a print room. At the end of each semester, the work of graduate art students is shown here. Just outside of the building is a four and a half-acre sculpture court. Two dozen pieces of sculpture by twentieth century artists including Rodin, Henry Moore and Matisse are displayed.

You can spend some peaceful moments in the Botanical Gardens. Rare shrubs, trees, flowers and ferns are beautifully arranged in a Japanese setting which is designed for quiet strolling. The special order of stone, wood and plant depicts natural scenes. This is primarily a research facility and is not always open to the public. It may be worth your while to check with campus authorities in advance and bicycle to the garden during visiting hours.

Hilgard Avenue leads out of the campus and into Westwood Village. This quaint community may cause you to forget you're in a large city. There are several snack shops and restaurants to choose from. A quick and delicious sandwich at Poppy's will

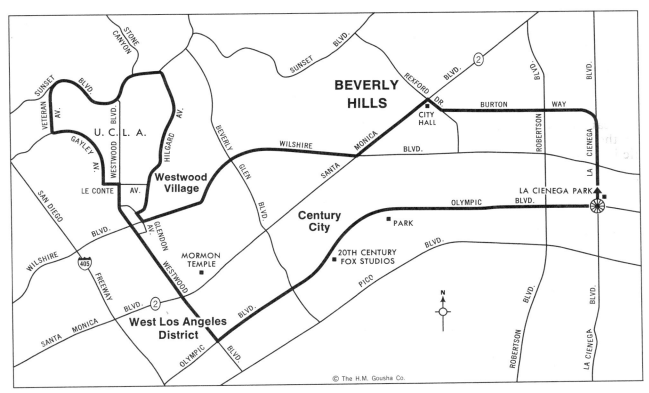

© The H.M. Gousha Co.

appease your appetite. Or you may enjoy the stained glass windows and friendly atmosphere that accompany the good food at Alice's Restaurant. After lunch, you may browse through the wares at nearby shops

The last leg of the journey takes you along Wilshire Boulevard and through Los Angeles Country Club. In order to avoid the traffic on Wilshire, turn left at Santa Monica Boulevard to Burton Way and back down La Cienega to the park where the trip began.

If you still have strength left and want to extend your day of cycling, see pages 12 and 13 for another tour with the same starting point.

Griffith Park—and Sidelights

Approx. mileage: 25

Rating: B

Terrain: Some uphill sections, but none too difficult for the beginner.

Best times for touring: This route may be traveled all year round. It is not recommended during the work week because of the hazards involved with heavy traffic. Weekends, especially Sundays, are best.

This ride leads to and through the nation's largest city park. Within 4,000 acres of Griffith Park are riding stables, golf courses, archery ranges, cricket fields, tennis courts, picnic areas and a bird sanctuary. Along the route you will pass some famous show business landmarks.

Starting from La Cienega Park on La Cienega Boulevard at Olympic, ride up to Beverly Boulevard. Here is C.B.S. Television City, the production center of many popular television programs. There are free tours Monday through Saturday. You can spend half an hour viewing studios, program sets, equipment and wardrobe departments.

(Note: Farmers Market is not on the tour route, but you may want to take a few extra minutes and visit it anyway. Despite being overrun by tourists, this is still one of the great markets of all time. You can pick up any number of good things for a picnic lunch, or buy a hot meal to eat on the spot.)

The route turns north on Vermont Avenue, past L.A. City College and Barnsdall Park to Los Feliz Boulevard. Coast down the hill into Griffith Park, where a whole collection of good places awaits you. With luck, you may be greeted with the sounds of an open air concert—a fitting start to your adventures in the park.

If you haven't picked up something for lunch, do so now so you will be equipped for a proper picnic later on.

The Observatory can be reached via a short side trip. En route, you pass the Greek Theatre. This summer showplace is a copy of the classic outdoor theatres of ancient Greece.

You may park your bicycle and enter the Observatory free of charge to view the exhibits. In the Planetarium, shows are presented daily except Mondays. For the price of $1.00, you can go to the moon, to a distant planet, see the northern lights, or watch the sun rise and set in an hour's time.

The Los Angeles Zoo is home to more than 3,000 animals in a beautiful arrangement of natural habitats. Birds of all varieties can be seen in one of the world's largest bird farms. The main zoo is on a hillside which requires some strenuous walking, but the guided tram is available if all you want is an overall view.

In the Children's Zoo, baby animals and barnyard creatures may be closely viewed and petted. There is a sea lion pool, prairie dog village and a nursery for animal mothers and their newborn babies.

Traveltown contains a large collection of transportation equipment including historic trains, planes and vintage automobiles. There is a unique multispeed tricycle as well as an operating railroad built to 1/5 scale.

When leaving Griffith Park via Forest Lawn Drive, you may look up to see the huge iron gates which easily identify Forest Lawn Memorial Park. These 306 landscaped acres accommodate weddings as well as funerals. The gardens are open daily from 9:00 a.m. to 5:30 p.m. Visitors may not only see the gravestones of famous people, but also somewhat edited replicas of famous works of art by Michelangelo.

Continue along Barham Blvd. to Cahuenga Blvd. West. This is a pleasant ride. The road is lightly traveled, mainly because the nearby freeway siphons off all of the through traffic. The Hollywood Bowl can be seen on the right. This is a beautiful natural amphitheater where summertime symphonies, pop music and soloists are presented.

The last leg of the route takes you along Highland Avenue through the Hollywood District down to Olympic Boulevard and back to La Cienega Park.

For another route with the same start-stop point, see pages 10 and 11.

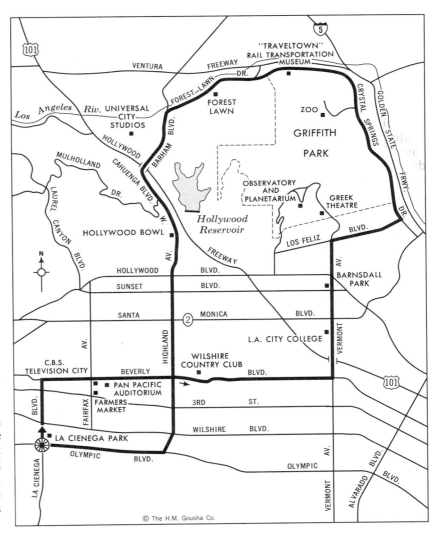

© The H.M. Gousha Co.

Beach, Mountain and Valley Tour

Approx. mileage: 46

Rating: A

Terrain: An all terrain ride—the beach, coastal mountains and some of San Fernando Valley. The hill climbs are rugged in places. Heavy traffic on coast and in cities.

Best times for touring: The route may be comfortably ridden on all but the hottest days of the year.

Definitely not for the novice rider, this tour has considerable scenic interest to compensate for the hills. You should be up to hill climbing on a multispeed bicycle.

Starting in Santa Monica from Lincoln Park (Lincoln and California Streets), a quick downhill run lets the rider out on the Coast Highway (State 1). This is a favorite of cyclists—not only a paved shoulder but also ocean breezes.

Santa Monica Beach State Park is always thronged. A few miles north Will Rogers State Park stretches smoothly beneath the towering Pacific Palisades. From here up the coast you hit a series of fine beaches —Las Tunas, Surfriders Beach, Malibu Lagoon State Beach Park. The rolling hills make this ride doubly interesting— if more difficult.

At Malibu turn onto Malibu Canyon Road, which will provide not only a change from the beach scenery but some exercise as well. The Santa Monica Mountains have a rugged beauty all their own although not forested at lower levels.

There is a major junction just about at the mountain crest where Malibu Canyon Road becomes Las Virgenes Road as it drops down into the valley. Mulholland Highway intersects here. Turn right on it and ride over the mountains on this good bicycling road, usually lightly traveled. This is part of the same, but more famous, Mulholland *Drive*. Ultimately you join Old Topanga Canyon Road, pick up Mulholland Drive and ride down into the San Fernando Valley.

A short detour west at the foot of the valley leads to the community of Calabasas. Retaining some old-time flavor and architecture, it is a good town to relax in and poke around a bit. Pick up the frontage road along U.S. 101 (it soon becomes Avenue San Luis) and follow it to Topanga Canyon Blvd. Here are plenty of places to stop for a hamburger before you start back over the hills.

The route leads straight back to the coast. Or, you may prefer to backtrack, picking up part of Mulholland Highway and Old Topanga Canyon Road in order to avoid traffic. Both are good bike routes.

Once back on Coast Highway the welcome ocean breezes help push you along. For an interesting entrance into Santa Monica turn onto Sunset Blvd. Then Chautauqua and W. Channel Road take you up to Ocean Avenue. From there it is an easy shot into Santa Monica and Lincoln Park.

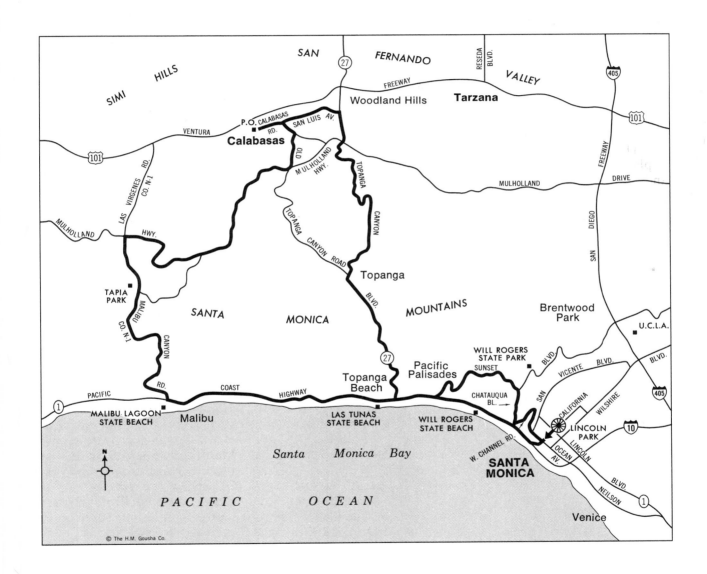

Calabasas Special Tour

Approx. mileage: 24

Rating: C

Terrain: Slightly rolling foothill roads as well as flat residential streets.

Best times for touring: This ride is good any time of year except on the hottest days.

This pleasant tour takes you through the southeastern end of the San Fernando Valley. The 24-mile trip should be very satisfactory for bicyclists with little experience and multi-speed bikes.

Drive Ventura Freeway (U.S. 101) to Reseda and Ventura Blvds. in Tarzana, your starting point. Following the route south and then west you find yourself meandering along interesting roads in the Santa Monica Mountains foothill region. Follow the streets in this order: Mecca, Wells Drive, Poe, Quedo Drive, Serrania Avenue, Dumetz Road, De La Osa, Capulin, Llano, and then Avenue San Luis.

This scenic warm-up through Woodland Hills leads to the picturesque community of Calabasas, the westernmost point on the route. Calabasas has retained some of the quaintness of the past. Take time out for a rest and refreshments here.

Then follow the route across U.S. 101 at Mulholland Drive and ride along Ventura Blvd., wide with only moderate traffic. A left turn on Shoup Avenue takes you out into the flat residential section of the valley. A number of parks are on the route, or close to it. They are good rest stops, as is Pierce Junior College, located on Victory Blvd.

Leave Victory Blvd. at Cor-

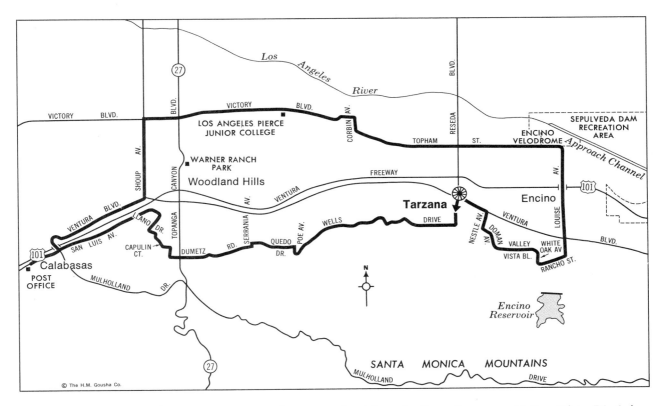

bin Avenue and later turn left on Topham Street. Continue along the route to the vast Sepulveda Dam Recreation Area. The point of interest for you is the Encino Velodrome. This is one of the finest bicycling tracks in the country. Frequent-ly, racing may be viewed. Or top riders may be seen working out on the track.

After watching the Velodrome activities and heading back to the roads, remember that *you* are not one of those racers yet. Take it easy as you head back to the hill roads. As the name Valley Vista Blvd. im-plies, there are excellent views of the valley on a smogless day. Stay on the route back to Ventura Blvd. and your starting place in Tarzana.

San Fernando Valley Park Tour

Approx. mileage: 25

Rating: C

Terrain: Slightly hilly in spots; mostly flat.

Best times for touring: A good easy tour most of the year, except on hot or smoggy days.

Some of the most pleasant parks in San Fernando Valley are mileposts of this easy tour. It is an interesting, relaxing ride for cyclists of all capabilities. San Fernando Valley weather is good cycling climate for all but the hottest days of summer.

A good starting place is Lanark Park, just north of the city of Canoga Park. You can park your car near the corner of Topanga Canyon Blvd. and Lanark Street. From there, ride the route south along Topanga Canyon to Saticoy Street (both are heavily traveled). Turn west and head for Woodlake Avenue and Roscoe Blvd., which takes you to the Orcutt Ranch Park.

Orcutt Ranch, a pleasant first-rest stop, has lawns, winding paths and interesting plant-life typical of the area. From there, loop around the big Chatsworth Reservoir on Valley Circle Blvd. You pass through gentle hills with grazing horses, taking Plummer Street, Shoup Avenue, Devonshire and Santa Susana into the town of Chatsworth.

Until just a few years ago, this was ranchland dotted with groves of orange trees. Now it is rapidly being occupied by contemporary settlers. This entire area has been a favorite Western movie-making spot, and Chatsworth Park, off to the west, has had its rocky hills shown in many a Saturday serial.

Continue on the tour, turning off Chatsworth Street on Mason. Mason Park, in the Porter Ranch area, provides another good resting place. Then, off to the rolling country along the north edge of the Valley. Follow

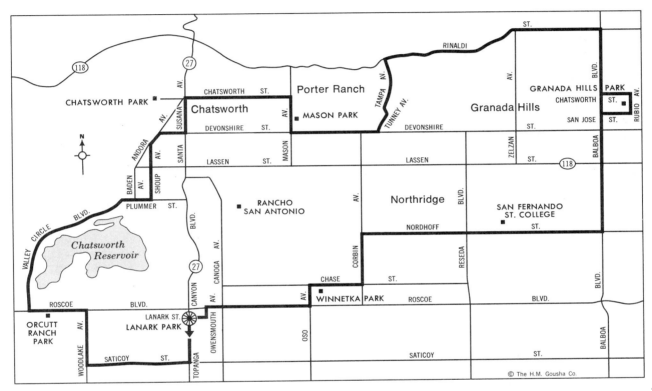

this route: Devonshire, left on Tunney and left on Des Moines. Pick up Rinaldi and follow it to Balboa Blvd.

When passing through Granada Hills, a left turn onto Chatsworth takes you to Granada Hills Park, where you can eat a picnic lunch. There also are restaurants along the route. Back to Balboa and down to Nordhoff Street, named for one of the area's early families.

On Nordhoff will be seen the campus of San Fernando State College. The last rest stop is at Winnetka Park on Chase Street. Then follow the route back to the starting place at Lanark Park.

"Lucky" Baldwin's Gardens and "Blue Boy"

Approx. mileage: 30

Rating: B

Terrain: Steep hills at the northern end of the loop.

Best times for touring: This ride is good on any day of the year providing the smog is not too heavy.

This is a pleasant ride through San Marino and into Santa Anita Canyon. Your trip begins at Alhambra Park on Alhambra and Palm, and the first section of the ride is along Huntington Drive in San Marino.

One of the greatest attractions in Los Angeles County is the Huntington Library and Art Gallery. For this interesting side-trip, ride up San Marino Avenue and Stratford. This was once a private estate owned by Henry Huntington who willed it to the public. The most famous painting is Gainborough's "Blue Boy." In the library you will see a collection of 250,000 rare books.

The extensive Botanical Gardens in the Huntington estate include ten acres of cactus and succulents, seven acres of camellias, 200 species of palms and a Japanese garden.

Back on the route, you will turn north as you pass Santa Anita Park. The thoroughbred horse racing season runs from December 26 to mid-April; the traffic may be heavy at this time of the year. If you do plan to pass by during the racing season, be at the track between 8 and 10 a.m. when you can watch the early morning workout session. Enjoy a continental breakfast served at the rail while trainers and jockeys prepare the horses for the afternoon races.

Just across Baldwin Avenue is the Los Angeles State and County Arboretum. The home of Comstock Lode millionaire "Lucky" Baldwin in the late 1880's, he developed the 127 acres into a beautifully landscaped arboretum. Here you may see some of the world's largest palm trees, thousands of exotic plants from all over.

After a rest at the Arboretum, you will begin a gradual climb up Santa Anita Avenue. You will encounter the real hills where Santa Anita Avenue becomes Santa Anita Canyon. Once you have made the grade, you will find that the scenery has made the struggle worthwhile. At the end of the road is the starting point for the hikers and backpackers. There are no stores in the Canyon, so bring along some energy food to restore your strength.

The return trip will provide an exciting downhill run and then excellent routing through Sierra Madre and into Pasadena. The trail is routed along Colorado, the scene of the annual Tournament of Roses Parade. If the traffic seems heavy, drop down a few blocks to Del Mar Boulevard. In either case, you will have a view of Pasadena City College. On Hill Avenue you will pass the California Institute of Technology. Many Nobel prize winners have studied and taught at this famous education center.

The last part of the ride takes you through San Marino, past Lacy Park and back to Alhambra Park.

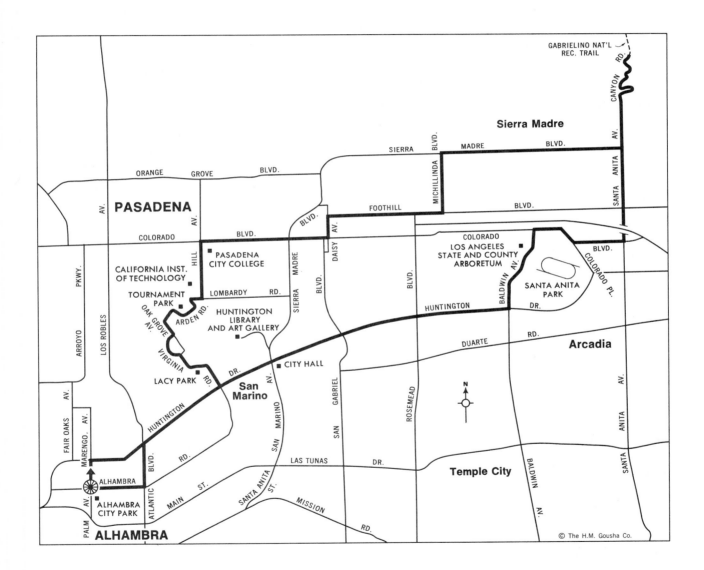

From Queen Mary to Buena Park

Approx. mileage: 37

Rating: B

Terrain: Well-paved, flat roads.

Best times for touring: Any day of the year.

This is a casual, easy tour of the Long Beach area highlighted by a visit to the Queen Mary and a later excursion to Knott's Berry Farm and other amusement centers in Buena Park.

Starting from El Dorado Park, the rider will tour past parks and down roads near the ocean. In the Belmont Pier area are many interesting streets where ocean lovers may stop and view the sea.

Bluff Park provides another excellent location to relax. You can buy refreshments at the Nu-Pike Amusement Park and go on some of the rides which provide a good aerial view of the coast. For art lovers, there is the museum at the east end of Bluff Park. It has a permanent exhibit of paintings, sculpture and art objects which emphasize Southern California artists.

If you have a couple of hours to spare, you may want to go down to pier J where the Queen Mary is docked. This great Cunard luxury liner was retired to the Long Beach Harbor on December 9, 1967. The ship is gradually being converted into a floating hotel, cafe, shopping complex, and museum.

Follow the Los Angeles River past pleasant residential areas and several country clubs. For the aircraft buff, be sure to stop at the Long Beach Airport where you can see a collection of vintage airplanes.

Ride on through the Lakewood Country Club area to Buena Park where you may choose to visit one or more of the following attractions.

First on the route is Japanese Deer Park. These tranquil grounds are modeled after a deer park in Nara, Japan. Over 200 tame deer roam the park. They are very affectionate and enjoy being fed and petted by daily visitors. There is also a seal feeding show, bear show, Karate demonstrations, dolphin show, tea ceremony, and Japanese

dancing. Other creatures living in the park include peacocks, Akita dogs, golden carp, and black swans. You can browse through the shops and the Great Teahouse of the Moon.

If you want to see some of your favorite film stars, go to the Movieland Wax Museum. More than 125 stars are recreated in wax in settings which depict the studios or sets from movies these actors made famous. There is an admission charge of $2.25.

Another lively attraction is the California Alligator Farm. Here is the home of over 3,000 alligators, crocodiles, lizards, snakes, tortoises, and turtles. Included in the collection is the world's largest crocodile in captivity. This Nile crocodile is about 15 feet in length and weighs over 1,400 pounds. The farm is open all year round, but if you go in the winter you may be disappointed to find many of these animals hibernating.

Across the street from the alligators is Knott's Berry Farm and Ghost Town. The atmos-

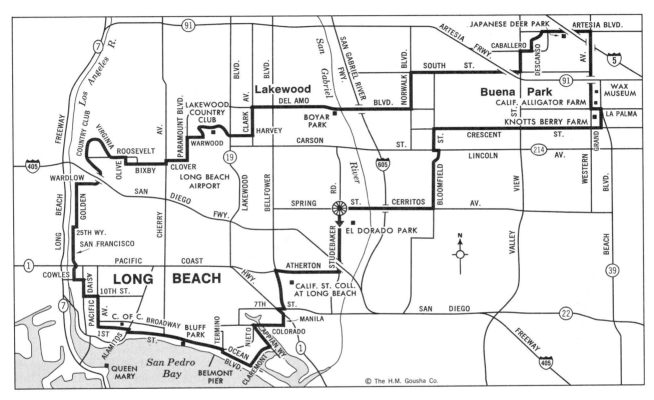

© The H.M. Gousha Co.

phere here is strictly old West. You can ride the Butterfield Stagecoach, pan for gold, visit the Indian trading post, and enjoy the melodrama at the Birdcage Theatre.

The Ghost Town is an authentic reminder of the early gold rush days of California. Independence Hall, the most recent exhibition, is a full-scale model of Independence Hall in Philadelphia. The 120 acres which comprise Knott's Berry Farm started as a roadside shed where boysenberries were sold. You can still find plenty of boysenberry tarts, pies, jams, and sherbets in the restaurants and shops. Mrs. Knott's chicken dinners are famous and delicious. You may want to try some before completing your journey. Cycle on through the Orange County area, looping back over easy roads to the starting place at El Dorado Park.

History Loop in Orange County

Approx. mileage: 28

Rating: C

Terrain: Flat

Best times for touring: Good any time of the year. Roads are least traveled on weekends, but suitable for weekdays, too.

This ride takes you through Yorba Linda, birthplace of President Richard Nixon and an area rich in history. California State College at Fullerton is a good starting point; it is adjacent to the Orange Freeway (State 57).

This area shows up often in the history of Los Angeles. The great Spanish explorer Juan Bautista de Anza followed the Santa Ana River when he brought hundreds of men, women and children from Sonora, Mexico, across the desert and into the fertile fields of California. Yorba Linda takes its name from the Yorba family, one of the first to settle here.

South of the Santa Ana River is an unexpected cycling bonus. What was once the main highway through Santa Ana Canyon is now bypassed, so it is nothing more than a well-paved, dead

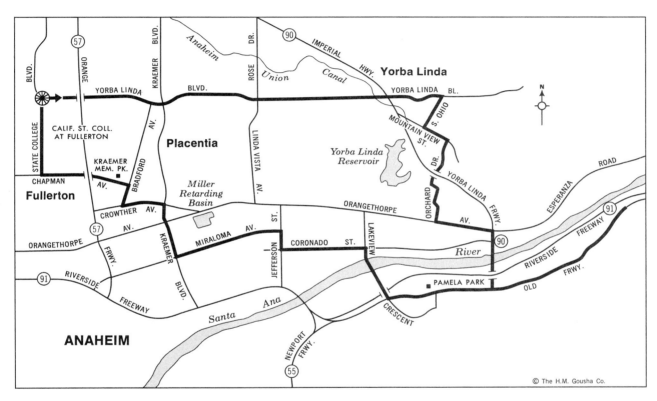

end road that makes a fantastic bike path. It doesn't go anywhere, but you can enjoy a leisurely up-and-back ride that is free of traffic hazards.

As you ride this loop, note the remaining pieces of irrigation channels. Water is the lifeblood of this dry country, and irrigation has always been critical to the success of the rich citrus and avocado industries that have contributed so much to the southern California economy.

Pamela Park makes an ideal stopping point before the trip back to the college campus. The park has both picnicking and camping facilities, and is well set up for bicyclists. However, there are no stores in the immediate area, so you'll have to carry lunch in from some other point.

Cucamonga Vineyard Special

Approx. mileage: 41

Rating: B

Terrain: Flat roads.

Best times for touring: Excellent cycling area when the temperature isn't too high and the wind is not too strong. Traffic is light any day of the week, all times of the year.

The vineyards in the heart of Southern California's sweet dessert wine country are unusual features of this moderate 41-mile tour.

The route starts at Archibald Avenue and San Bernardino Avenue near the town of Guas-ti. Ride on to Haven Avenue, turn left and cruise along this good flat road to Cucumonga, a town that Jack Benny helped make famous over thirty years ago on his radio show. Cucamonga also has the distinction of being the home of the oldest crop in the state. The mission fathers planted wine grapes in the valley in 1804 and Southern California's first winery was established at Cucamonga in 1859. City sprawl is diminishing the vineyards but nearly 19,000 acres are still devoted to grapes that chiefly produce sweet dessert wines.

As you ride through the wine country, signs will be seen that invite you to some of the many excellent wine tasting rooms. Many are centered on Foothill Boulevard. Don't hesitate to drop in for a bit of refreshment, but, if you are under age, you will be served grape juice.

Turn right off Haven Avenue on Base Line Road, which was the key reference line for the early surveyors who mapped California. Take Etiwanda Avenue left through the town of Etiwanda on to Highland Avenue. After turning right it is only about seven miles to lunch and the town of Rialto. A recommended eating spot is Sage's, located at Foothill and Riverside Avenue.

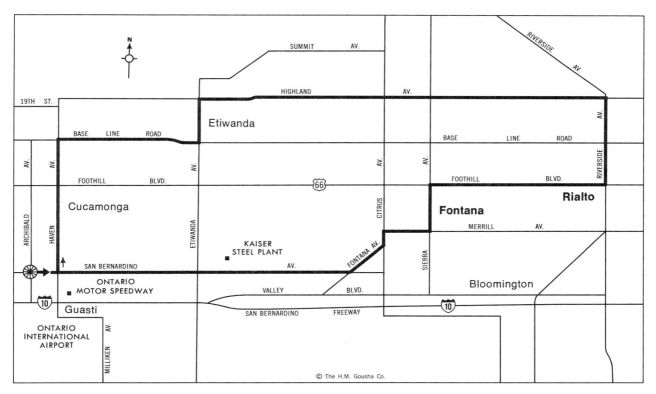

© The H.M. Gousha Co.

After lunch, cruise west on Foothill to Sierra Avenue. Turning south you will cross the Pacific Electric Railway, pass through the town of Fontana and ride over the Atchison, Topeka and Santa Fe tracks.

Ride right on Merrill Avenue for a short distance, turn onto Cirtur for only a brief time and take Fontana Avenue to San Bernardino Avenue. Travel on west past the huge Kaiser steel plant, the largest in the West.

Just a bit southwest of your starting point near Guasti is Ontario International Airport. If you are a plane owner, you can just load in your bike and fly home. Regardless, the airport is a fascinating point of interest.

Upland—Down and Around

Approx. mileage: 48

Rating: B

Terrain: Flat land, rural, tree-lined roads.

Best times for touring: Any time of year except summer is good for this excellent tour. There is little traffic, especially on weekends.

Contrasts on this tour are interesting—airports and country quiet roads. You will pass near three large airports on your trip from Upland down to quaint old Arlington, around Corona to Norco, and back.

Get on your bike near the Trail of the Madonna Monument at Foothill Blvd. and Euclid Avenue in Upland (a gateway to the Mount Baldy recreational area).

Ride down Euclid to Ontario and turn left onto Mission Blvd. (State 60). You will soon be riding alongside the big Ontario International Airport. On down the road a bit you will notice the Mira Loma Air Force Station. Shortly past this, the road becomes Van Buren Blvd. and soon takes you past Paradise Knolls Golf Course and the Riverside Airport.

Cruise on into the pleasant old town of Arlington which has managed to maintain a quaint rural identity. Magnolia Avenue is well named, although palms are also plentiful. The value of an "old road" will be appreciated as you ride along this tree shaded lane, little traffic to cope with and the Riverside Freeway in clear view, all the way to Corona.

Lunch time. Corona has many satisfactory spots; try Scotties on Main Street. One of the world's leading lemon producers, Corona is also at the mouth of the Santa Ana Canyon.

After a rest, it will be an easy ride up Hamner Avenue through Norco. Shortly after crossing the Santa Ana River, you will turn left on Cloverdale Road. Ride up Archibald past the Ontario Golf Club and take Philadelphia Street back to Euclid Avenue. This pepper-tree flanked street is wide, handsome, and seven miles long. Each summer it is the scene of the famous All States Picnic with a table stretching out for a mile.

Ontario is also noted as center for winemaking and citrus production. The surrounding countryside is studded with groves and vineyards.

Retrace the early part of the tour back to your starting place in Upland.

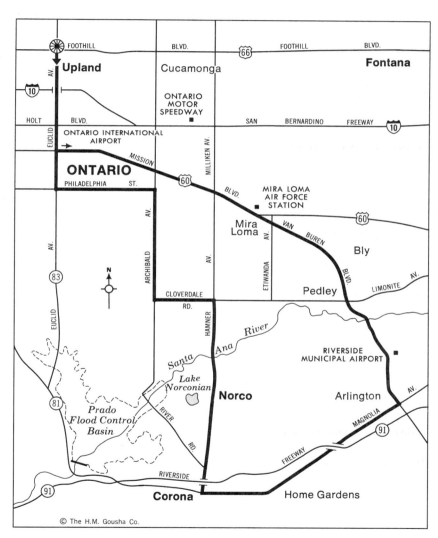

© The H.M. Gousha Co.

29

Ride into History and Roses

Approx. mileage: 28

Rating: B

Terrain: Excellent roads, mostly flat.

Best times for touring: This route may be ridden any time of the year, except for smoggy days. Traffic is light, even on weekends.

Historic early California and thousands of blooming rose bushes are bonuses on this short tour in the area of Pico Rivera and La Puente.

To reach the departure point at Washington and Norwalk Blvds. take San Gabriel River Freeway (Int. 605) to Washington and drive east a half mile.

Get on your bike and head north on Norwalk Blvd. At the intersection with Whittier Boulevard you will have to make the decision whether or not to go a half mile out of your way to visit the ranch home of Pio Pico, California's last Mexican governor. If you decide on the loop tour, you will learn something of California's early history at Pio Pico's hacienda, 6003 Pioneer Blvd. The old house has a wine cellar, some of the original furniture, a grape arbor and a wall section that has been cut away to show the strength and details of building. The monument is open from 9 a.m. to 5 p.m. except Monday, Tuesdays, and holidays.

Resume your tour on Norwalk making an easy left turn on to Workman Mill Road. Within a few blocks you will be in the midst of Rose Hills Memorial Park. Any time of the year you will visit the grounds and be able to see blooms, but during the peak blossoming times in spring and fall, you will be dazzled by literally hundreds of varieties—old familiar roses, new varieties and specimens rare in size and color.

From here, wind along Workman Mill Road, crossing over the diversion channel of the San Gabriel River. Turn left on Coleford, right on rossmont and left again on Fairplain picking up Basetdale Avenue, with a few old structures still there.

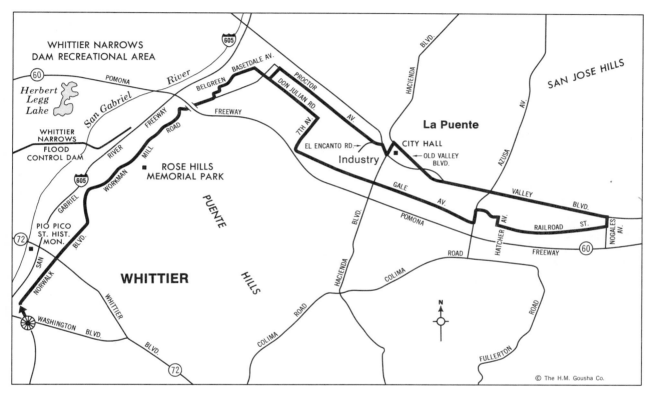

While riding along Proctor, turn right for a block on El Encanto to the sanitarium. From the end of this short lane you can see the Temple Hacienda, a century-old residence of early landowners. In the family mausoleum are inscribed many names of early landholders, including Pio Pico, Temple, and Rowland. The hacienda is not open to the public but historical societies are trying to preserve the famous landmark.

Ride through part of La Puente on Old Valley Blvd. Then pick up the bigger Valley Blvd. and continue along the Southern Pacific tracks to Nogales Avenue. Here you'll find a good spot for lunch and a rest.

After lunch you will wind back along lightly traveled roads to Workman Mill Road and finally to your starting point.

Lions, a Ferry Boat and Old Cars

Approx. mileage: 40

Rating: B

Terrain: Moderate hills to the coast. Excellent terrain all the way.

Best times for touring: Excellent trip for any but the hottest days of summer.

Thousands of boats, a ferry ride, lion country, old cars—the variety on this tour is tremendous. Basically, it is a somewhat difficult route from Tustin through interesting parts of Orange County, over moderate hills to the coast and up to Newport Beach.

The starting point in Tustin is at Red Hill Avenue and Laguna Road. Turn left off Laguna at Browning Avenue and follow along Bryan and Jeffrey Road, where you turn right and eventually cross over Interstate 5 (State 101).

Pick up Moulton Parkway which takes you to Lion Country Safari, the "zoo" where the animals are loose and visitors must stay in their cars with the windows rolled up. If you really want to feel close to rhinos and the like, rental cars are available at the entrance (primarily, these are for visitors who arrive in convertibles—the tops tend to cave in under the weight of a curious lion).

Follow Moulton Parkway to Valencia Road, which parallels Interstate 5, and ride south to Mission Viejo. Then cruise along south on La Paz Road to the intersection with Crown Valley Parkway.

The Parkway deadends at Coast Highway (State 1), which will take you along the Pacific north to Laguna Beach. The shore is lined with beach cottages, studios and shops of artists and craftsmen. Often, if you stop to look and shop you can watch the craftsmen at work on ceramic pots, weaving, and leather craft.

Way back in the late 1800's artists took to the Laguna bluffs to paint the beauty of the ocean front. Since 1913 when the colony first started displaying their works informally on fences and sides of houses, Laguna has been associated with arts and crafts.

North of Laguna Beach Highway 1 leaves the coast after a while and soon you will roll into the environs of Corona del Mar. Pass MacArthur Blvd. and Irvine Coast Country Club on your right. Leave Highway 1 at Marine Avenue and turn south toward the bay.

Almost immediately you will cross the busy yacht basin to Balboa Island and explore along Park Avenue. From Agate Avenue you take a novel trip on the ferry over to the Balboa peninsula for lunch. Perhaps you will want to walk along the beach or ride on the beachfront bike road.

From there you wind up Balboa Blvd. along the peninsula, where the action on both sides of you centers on surf and sail.

The beaches are classic and hundreds of craft call Newport Bay home.

Follow the route via Newport and Harbor Blvds. inland to Costa Mesa.

If you like old cars as well as bikes you are headed in the right direction. Ride out Harbor and Baker Street to the Briggs Cunningham Automotive Museum. Superb Rolls Royces, Mercedes—all the famed names in autos are here. (Open daily, 10-5.)

For the home stretch, ride along Red Hill and Main to Harvard Avenue where you will see the U.S. Marine Corps Air Facility, containing the huge hangers that were built years ago to house the militray dirigibles then used by the United States. Follow the route back to the starting point in Tustin.

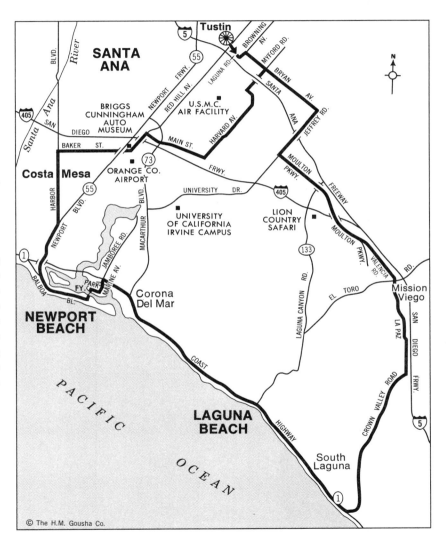

© The H.M. Gousha Co.

Huntington and Newport—Two-Harbor Tour

Approx. mileage: 35

Rating: B

Terrain: The ride is almost entirely flat. Half the tour follows the coastline.

Best times for touring: Southern California weather makes this a good trip all year round.

Cycle down the coast from beautiful Huntington Harbor to Newport Beach and back. An easy ride, this tour is suitable for any rider if the distance isn't too great.

Starting from 17th and Walnut Avenue, just off Pacific Coast Highway (State 1) in Huntington Beach, follow the route past Huntington High School and north on Golden West. On Warner you pass both the Meadowlark Golf Club and Meadowlark Airport before you reach Saybrook. Turn north on Saybrook and loop back to Davenport Drive.

Circle around the island for a look at the harbor and a brief rest before making your way back to Warner and out to the Coast Highway.

Southern California's famed coastline is your route south to Newport. Refineries and supply stations mar the scenery somewhat on the left, so keep your eyes toward the Pacific and its wildlife—surfers and girls.

Five miles down the coast is the Huntington Beach Municipal Pier. You'll know you're there by the traffic and the crowds. Sometimes waves break over 12 feet, and they break nicely—bringing surfers. Some of the best in the world work out here, and the Pier has been the site for large surfing championships.

The first signal after crossing the Santa Ana River is Orange Street. Turn left to Seashore Drive and ride down to 24th Street in Newport Beach. Jog over to Balboa Blvd. and stay on it down the peninsula to Main Street. Lots to eat in this area.

As you ride down the peninsula you are sandwiched between the Pacific and Newport Bay to your left.

For an alternate route south and a better view of the bay, plus some of the biggest sailboats and fanciest houses in wealthy Orange County, turn off Balboa on any side street to Bay Street. At Eighth turn right and go to Main Street.

Finish lunch and take in the Pavilion and amusement park area, if there is time. Two blocks back up Bay is Palm Avenue. Pass up the cars waiting for the ferry and take the special entrance for bikes.

The ferry boat ride is short but offers a chance to see the sailboats almost hit you. Sometimes the traffic jam on the water is as bad as the one on shore.

After a tour of Balboa Island wheel on down to Corona Del Mar State Beach, passing Balboa Yacht Club on the way. Poppy Avenue takes you to Coast Highway and out to the Corona Del Mar Freeway. Follow the route, passing the Orange County Airport and Movieland of the Air. Stop in for a view of antique aircraft. The final spurt on Adams Avenue directs you to 17th Avenue and the starting point.

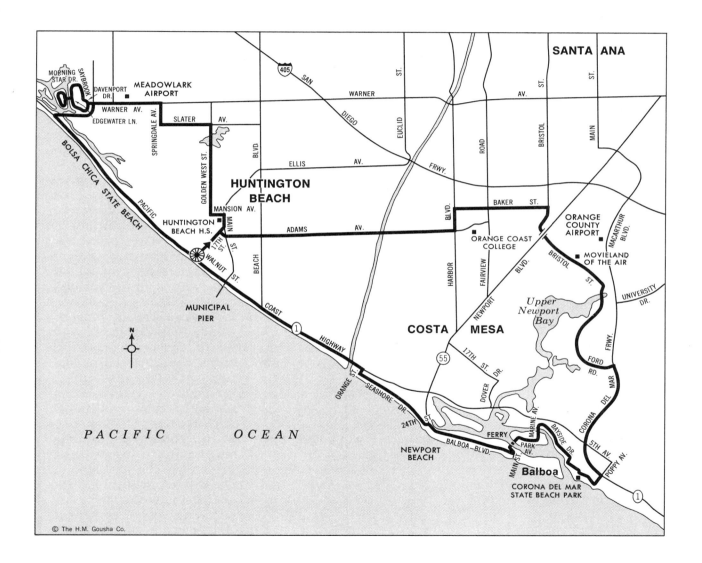

SANTA ANA

HUNTINGTON BEACH

MORNING STAR DR.
SAYBROOK
DAVENPORT DR.
MEADOWLARK AIRPORT
WARNER AV.
EDGEWATER LN.
SLATER AV.
SPRINGDALE AV.
GOLDEN WEST ST.
MANSION AV.
MAIN ST.
17TH ST.
WALNUT ST.
BEACH BLVD.
Huntington Beach H.S.
MUNICIPAL PIER

BOLSA CHICA STATE BEACH
PACIFIC

405
SAN DIEGO FRWY.
WARNER AV.
ELLIS AV.
ADAMS AV.
EUCLID ST.
ST.
BRISTOL ST.
MAIN ST.
AV.

BAKER ST.
HARBOR BLVD.
FAIRVIEW
NEWPORT BLVD.
BRISTOL ST.
ORANGE COAST COLLEGE
ORANGE COUNTY AIRPORT
MOVIELAND OF THE AIR
MACARTHUR BLVD.
UNIVERSITY DR.

COSTA MESA

Upper Newport Bay

55
17TH ST.
DOVER DR.
FORD RD.
CORONA DEL MAR FRWY.
5TH AV.
POPPY AV.

COAST HIGHWAY
1

ORANGE ST.
SEASHORE DR.
24TH ST.
BALBOA BLVD.
NEWPORT BEACH
FERRY
PARK AV.
MARINE AV.
MAIN ST.
BAYSIDE DR.
Balboa

CORONA DEL MAR STATE BEACH PARK
1

PACIFIC   OCEAN

N

© The H.M. Gousha Co.

35

San Juan Capistrano—Mission and Swallows

Approx. mileage: 30

Rating: B

Terrain: Mostly flat; a few rolling hills.

Best times for touring: Best to take this trip in the spring. The summer heat is terrible.

The quiet back roads are the ones to follow if you are riding to San Juan Capistrano. This route to one of California's loveliest old missions (and the summer home of thousands of the famous swallows) is a mild run on lightly traveled roads.

To start the tour, drive on Interstate 5 (Santa Ana Freeway) to the Sand Canyon Avenue exit for the old town of East Irvine. Make Moulton Parkway your route south.

Just after you cross Int. 405 (San Diego Freeway) you come to Lion Country Safari. Here are 500 acres of authentic wildlife preserve where African animals roam free. Even if you don't want to take the time to rent a car and drive the eight miles of jungle and plains trails that wind through strolling lions, you might enjoy the junior jungle with lion cubs and other baby animals.

Take Valencia Road over to Avenida de la Carlotta that parallels the freeway and goes past Leisure World. Ride on Mackenzie, making a jog finally on Pine and over to La Paz Road. Across the freeway is Mission Viejo that some California historians claim was the site of the original Capistrano mission. At the bottom of the hill, just before the freeway, turn right on Cabot Road. When you come to a barricade, walk or ride around it and down the steep hill. Later you have to walk your bike across the railroad tracks to reach the paved road, Camino Capistrano. Before you visit the mission you may want to stop for a hamburger at the stand across from San Juan Capistrano high school.

The fluttering pigeons, the color of the lush gardens enhance the mission. Pillars and arches in partial ruin due to time and the upheaval of the tremendous 1812 earthquake and many carefully restored buildings remain. This is one of the most beautiful of the missions and the Serra Chapel is still in use.

The famed swallows that leave the mission each October 23 for warmer winter roosts and return every March 19 put San Juan Capistrano into the news at least twice a year.

After your visit to the mission you may want to try some Mexican food in the city before you start the return ride.

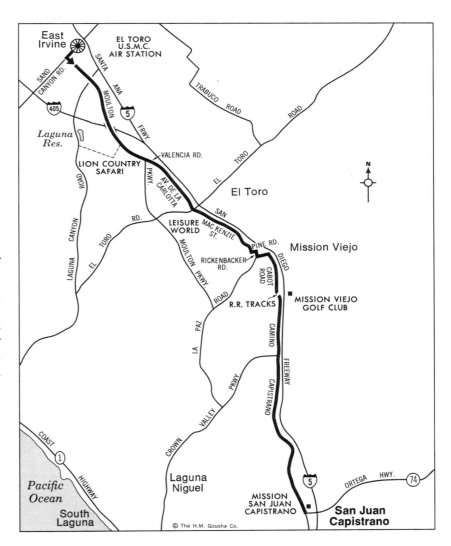

Up the San Gabriels to Mt. Baldy

Approx. mileage: 57

Rating: A

Terrain: Rugged roads with some straight-up climbs. Very little traffic on Glendora Ridge Road section.

Best times for touring: It is best to try this ride in spring or fall when the weather is mild. Summer heat is rather severe and in winter cars with skiers clutter the snow-covered road.

Buy survival food in advance. This ride is serious—and the places to purchase a snack once you are on the road are few and far between. Also, take along water.

Start this interesting but difficult ride from Azusa Avenue in Azusa. The city is soon left behind as the rider enters the San Gabriel Canyon. The rolling uphill route passes Morris Reservoir where there are evidences of past Navy testing.

Looking down from the canyon road you can see the river (or river bed, depending on the season) and an old road that unquestionably suffered from many spring rains. Looking up, you see the imposing and rugged San Gabriel peaks.

Eventually you make a gradual turn to the east along the East Fork of the San Gabriel. The recreation areas along the river will be filled with city folk escaping. A small restaurant at one of the campgrounds may be open for refreshment.

The end of the East Fork spells one thing—UP! A lively five-mile climb leads to Glendora Ridge Road. After a left turn you head straight for Mount Baldy. The ascent is less severe here.

Wildflowers and wildlife make the Ridge Road a choice run. It's hard to believe that this solitude with spacious views of the deep canyons is only about 45 air miles from the Los Angeles city hall. The gradual uphill climb will climax with a drop *down* into Mount Baldy Village, where there is a good lunch stop. On up the road is a fine ski area.

After a rest and some food, the downhill ride will be a thrill. You whip down Mt. Baldy Road and at times see sections of the old road that were washed out. The new road was built in 1955 but the older trail has a history as a wagon road and toll road. There was a time when the canyon experienced gold fever and this was the

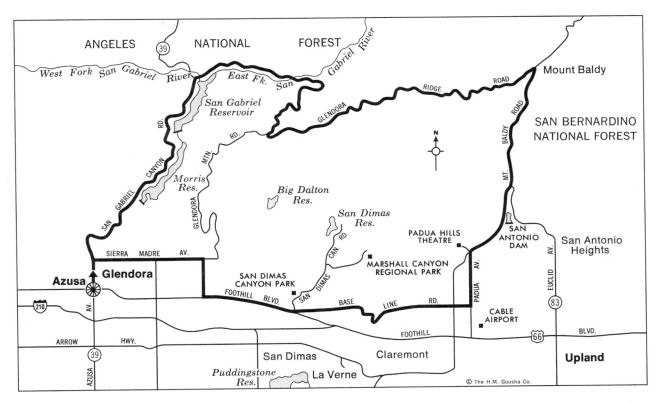

route to the diggings. This downhill run, like all others, should be negotiated cautiously. These are a thrill but require constant alertness.

Soon you pass orange groves and a dam. At Padua Avenue you may want to make a short side trip to Padua Hills Theater. There is a restaurant and an interesting Mexican shop.

At Base Line the route turns west over the rugged lowlands that are becoming populated. Base Line originally was the reference for surveyors who mapped this area. The route leads through Glendora and back to Azusa—the end of a *real* ride.

Earthquake Ride to Jackrabbit Trail

Approx. mileage: 36

Rating: B

Terrain: Rolling foothill country, excellent roads.

Best times for touring: Any season except summer is good for this ride.

The novice rider here has an opportunity to flavor the San Jacinto mountain range without struggling over the difficult peaks. Gradual uphill roads along an earthquake fault take you to the fringes of high country. Much of the homeward ride is downhill through scenic, rolling hills.

A good place to start this relatively easy 36 mile loop is in Hemet, which is reached by driving U. S. 395 south to State 74 and then east.

Famous for the annual spring Ramona pageant based on Helen Hunt Jackson's romantic story of early California, Hemet lies on the foothill slopes of the San Jacintos, amid flourishing fruit and walnut orchards, orange groves and acres of commercial rose plantings.

In Hemet, leave your car near the intersection of Florida Avenue and State Street. If you plan to snack along the foothill route, buy supplies and fill your water bottle before leaving town.

From Hemet ride out San Jacinto Avenue to the town of San Jacinto about three miles away. Both of these towns lie at an elevation of 1,500 feet and are supply centers for the Mount San Jacinto recreation area.

Picturesque and lightly traveled Soboba Road stays in the foothills through hot springs country. Actually, you are skimming along on an earthquake fault—the San Jacinto Fault runs along the base of the steep range. Located on this line are both Soboba and Gilman Hot Springs, desert resorts built where earthquake activity created hot springs.

The part of the road that winds along the San Jacinto River is located in a fault valley. Farther north of Soboba are areas where the perpendicular

change has been over 1,000 feet.

You'll commence a gradual uphill climb through Lamb Canyon on State 79.

Beaumont marks the halfway point of the trip and is a good place to stop for lunch. There are several satisfactory restaurants where you can stop for a meal and a rest before the homeward sprint.

After lunch ride west on State 60 to Jackrabbit Trail for a delightful trip down through the canyon. Be glad you are on a road named for jackrabbits—the steep adjoining hills are known as The Badlands.

After swooping down the canyon road you will join Foothills Road and will pass near another of the hot springs chain. A short road to the east leads to Eden Hot Springs near 2,353-foot high Mount Eden.

Follow along through the hills on the scenic Gilman Springs Road back to Hemet.

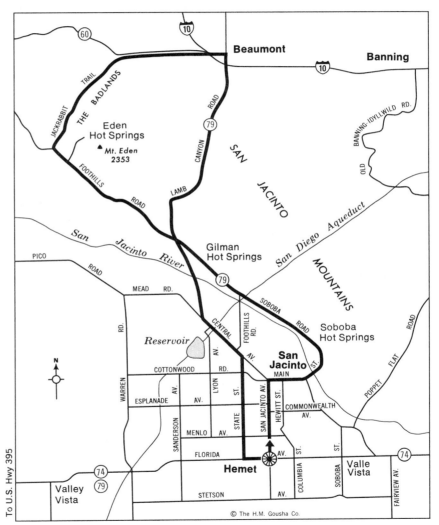

© The H.M. Gousha Co.

To Perris for Lunch

Approx. mileage: 45

Rating: B

Terrain: Rolling hills

Best times for touring: Excellent ride all year except during the hottest part of summer.

Starting near Elsinore, this 45-mile ride takes you through some of the real "country" remaining in the Los Angeles area. It is possible to plan a camping weekend around your bike tour, staying at the Lake Elsinore State Recreation Area. Campsites and camper facilities are available.

The tour starts at the north end of Lake Elsinore. Follow the route and join State 71, riding up through the Temescal Valley. This is rolling pastoral California countryside, dotted with chaparral and live oaks. If you stop at the Temescal Forest Station they can give you information about the Indian pictograms just a short side trip off the highway ahead.

Just as you turn right on Cajalco Road you will pass the Old Butterfield Stage Station. It was over this same route that the famous Butterfield Stage bumped along, bringing pre-Civil War travelers and mail to Los Angeles.

The rolling road directs you along Lake Mathews and past the old mining areas of Gavilan. You will see the Old Elsinore Road—take this to Perris for lunch. In this case, not Maxim's but the Frosty Freeze.

Perris, which dates back to 1886, was named by a railroad engineer, Fred T. Perris. Railroads still play a big part in Perris—The Orange Empire Trolley Museum is located a mile south of town on A Street. The yellow Trolley Museum signs in town will guide you to the site.

There is no admission to the ten-acre museum where you will see a San Francisco cable car and other old street cars, locomotives, a car from the Great Northern Railway of Eire. If you are a Sunday afternoon visitor you may be on time for a ride in one of the trolleys of a bygone era. You will note that these public transportation devices are also smog-free.

The hilly ride on State 74 back to Elsinore takes you in view of Steele Peak (elevation 2529 feet) and past the site of the Good Hope Mine. You will cross State Highway 71 shortly before completing the loop at the north shore of Lake Elsinore.

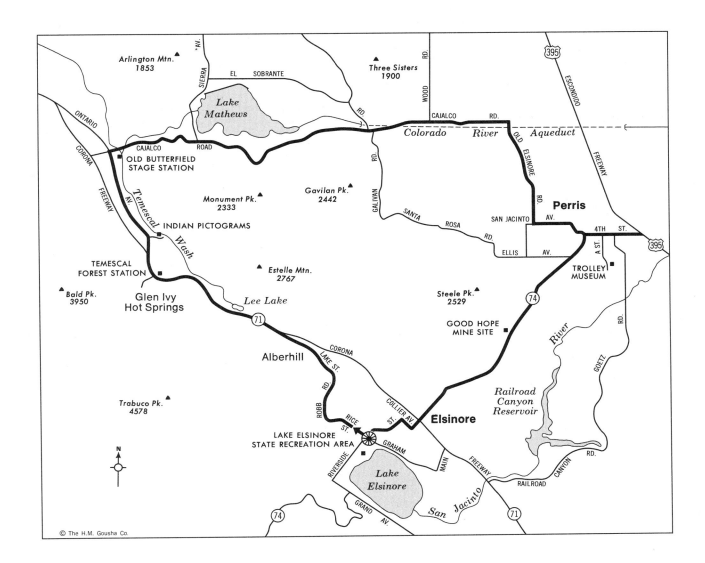

Arlington Mtn.
1853

EL SOBRANTE

Three Sisters
1900

SIERRA AV.

WOOD RD.

395

ESCONDIDO FREEWAY

Lake Mathews

ONTARIO

CAJALCO RD.

Colorado River Aqueduct

OLD ELSINORE RD.

CORONA FREEWAY

CAJALCO ROAD

OLD BUTTERFIELD
STAGE STATION

Temescal AV.

Monument Pk.
2333

Gavilan Pk.
2442

RD.

GALIVAN RD.

SANTA ROSA RD.

Perris

INDIAN PICTOGRAMS

Wash

SAN JACINTO AV.

4TH ST.

395

TEMESCAL
FOREST STATION

Estelle Mtn.
2767

ELLIS AV.

A ST.

TROLLEY
MUSEUM

Bald Pk.
3950

Glen Ivy
Hot Springs

Lee Lake

71

Steele Pk.
2529

74

River

Alberhill

CORONA

LAKE ST.

GOOD HOPE
MINE SITE

GOETZ RD.

Trabuco Pk.
4578

ROBB RD.

RICE ST.

COLLIER AV.

Elsinore

Railroad
Canyon
Reservoir

N

LAKE ELSINORE
STATE RECREATION AREA

GRAHAM

RIVERSIDE

Lake
Elsinore

MAIN

FREEWAY

RAILROAD

CANYON RD.

74

GRAND AV.

San Jacinto

71

© The H.M. Gousha Co.

43

Through Valleys of Beauty and Legend

Approx. mileage: 67

Rating: A

Terrain: Gradual uphill climbs, fast downhill runs through rolling valleys.

Best times for touring: Mild seasons.

This countryside, rich in legend, takes the cyclist from the flatland to elevations approaching 5,000 feet, and then on to breathtaking drops back to the lower desert region.

A good departure point is Hemet. You can park your car near Florida and San Jacinto Avenues. To reach Hemet, take Interstate 15, and turn on State Highway 74.

Heading east, the ride begins on the flat and casual egress road which permits warming up and checking the equipment.

Just south of Hemet and almost at the beginning of your ride, you will pass near Ramona Bowl. This outdoor theater is the home of the celebrated Ramona Outdoor Play, a yearly event that stages the legendary love story of Ramona and her Indian lover, Alessandro.

As you leave the area of the Bowl, pick up State 74 for a gradual uphill climb through the canyons with scenic views of the mountains and the valley to the west.

You will realize you're "getting high" when you look back to retrace your path. Traffic is normally very light and you should have no problems.

The next milestone you reach will be Mountain Center. This fork in the road boasts a country store well known to bicyclists as it provides a welcome stopping place for refreshment.

From here the route heads southeast, climbing slightly and then following a high valley. This is beautiful country, with the foliage and broad grassy areas typical of the mile-high altitude. It is also an area of colorful folklore.

Soon after passing Keen Camp Summit, elevation 4,917, you will enter the Garner Valley, the historical setting of much of the Ramona legend.

As you leave the Garner Valley you will pass Thomas Mountain, the site of many precious gem finds. From the gemstones you travel to Paradise, the valley—not the one in the sky. Paradise Valley (pick up State 71) is your jumping off spot for the land below. The high mountain valley now gives way to excellent downhill runs into the community of Anza. The 1,000 foot drop is great.

When you leave Anza, an old Indian rancheria, and head for Aguanga, you will be retracing the first route into the San Jacinto Mountain country.

At Aguanga the route continues to Radec where the rider again encounters adventuresome canyon runs on Sage Road (R-3). The terrain in this area is especially interesting. Rugged plant life abounds that is capable of withstanding bitter winter cold and torrid summer heat. The route leads past Magee Hills, through Sage and into St. Johns Canyon.

Soon the road will become quite flat and straighten out into a typical desert road. This heralds the approach of Hemet, and the end of the ride.

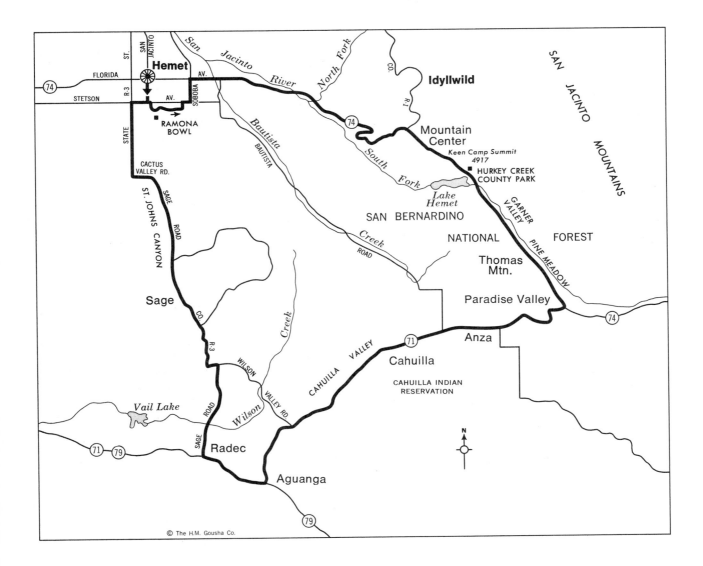

Hemet

Idyllwild

SAN JACINTO MOUNTAINS

FLORIDA

STETSON

RAMONA BOWL

Mountain Center

Keen Camp Summit 4917

HURKEY CREEK COUNTY PARK

Lake Hemet

SAN BERNARDINO

NATIONAL

FOREST

GARNER VALLEY

PINE MEADOW

Thomas Mtn.

Paradise Valley

CACTUS VALLEY RD.

ST. JOHNS CANYON

SAGE ROAD

Sage

Creek

ROAD

CO. R-3

WILSON

VALLEY RD.

CAHUILLA VALLEY

Anza

Cahuilla

CAHUILLA INDIAN RESERVATION

Vail Lake

SAGE ROAD

Wilson Creek

Radec

Aguanga

N

© The H.M. Gousha Co.

Through the Land of Forbidden Fruits

Approx. mileage: 35

Rating: B

Terrain: Steep hills and long downhill runs.

Best times for touring: Spring or fall are best. If the weather is cool, bring warm clothing for the downhill ride.

The starting point for this tour is Redlands. Named for its red soil, this quiet city is the hub of adjacent agricultural areas. The 15,000 acres of orange groves surrounding the town make Redlands the world's largest shipper of navel oranges. Take the San Bernardino Freeway (U.S. 10) to the Orange Street (State 106) turnoff in Redlands, turn left under the freeway and park along Orange near Redlands Blvd.

The ride begins along rather lightly traveled roads. The first turn is a right on Lugonia Avenue (also State 38). On your right will be the University of Redlands. Founded in 1907 by the Northern Baptist Convention, the hundred-acre campus now enrolls about 1,400 students. An unusual building here is an octagonal granite museum housing a Lincoln memorial with artifacts and relics of the former president's life. It is the only memorial of its kind west of the Mississippi. The university also maintains an outdoor theater in Smiley Park, a formal garden of 400 acres with exotic trees and shrubs from all over the world.

Continuing along the route you will pass the community of Mentone. Further along is a fish hatchery which is an interesting rest stop.

Just down the road from the hatchery take a right on Bryant and, after a short distance, ride left on Oak Glen Road. You now begin to climb—a good chance for a workout for the capable rider or, if you feel like relaxing, to walk your bike and admire the scenery.

Oak Glen will be reached at an elevation of 4,846 feet, a good climb from the starting height of 1,357 feet. At Oak Glen you can rest your legs and let your nose do all the work. Something sure smells good here. This is apple country, the home of some of the most delicious apples, cider and apple pie in the world.

During September and October some very famous names in the apple world ripen on the trees of Oak Glen. Gravenstein, McIntosh, Jonathan, Red Delicious, Rome Beauties and one variety for which the Glen is famous, the Golden Delicious, all grow in these fertile hills.

The Johnny Appleseed of this area, according to oldtimers, was Joe Wilshire who staked his claim here in 1876 and planted the first tree. With the birth of each baby in the Wilshire family he planted new acreage. Mt. Wilshire, one of a group of mountains that overlook the Glen was named after Joe Wilshire.

There are several restaurants in the town of Oak Glen but if you're after apple pie try the Pieloon. The remainder of the

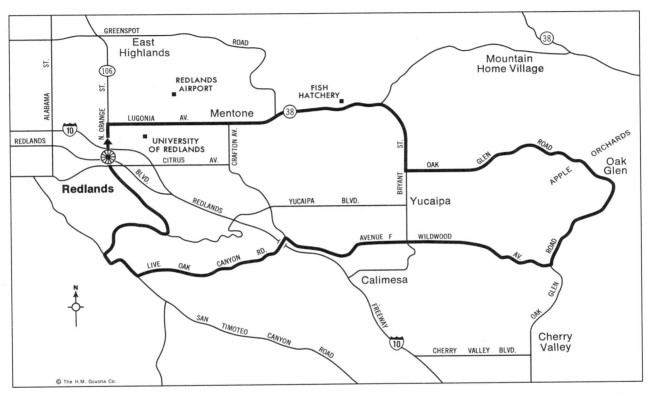

© The H.M. Gousha Co.

trip is downhill so don't be afraid to really dig into that food. Also, if you have the time you might want to browse around the gift and candy shops.

After lunch follow the route down Oak Glen Road. This is an exciting downhill run. Have fun, but watch the turns.

After dropping down the hill about three miles take a right on Wildwood into Avenue F and cross the freeway to Live Oak Canyon Road. Over railroad tracks turn right on San Timoteo Canyon Road; right again on the first paved road, Alessandro. A right on Crescent, left on Center, another right on Brookside will take you back to Redlands and your car.

High Desert Loop to Big Pines Country

Approx. mileage: 60

Rating: A

Terrain: High desert to tall pines. A climb of about 3,000 feet.

Best times for touring: A tour for the mild seasons; too hot during summer, snow in winter. Traffic is light.

Varying terrain—a chance to see the desert transformed into mighty pines—is the highpoint of this loop tour through the Antelope Valley area.

The starting point is Littlerock. Take State Route 14 to Palmdale, turn right on State 138 and Littlerock lies ten miles ahead. The ride follows the Fort Tejon Road through typical "high desert" terrain to Valyermo where there is a ranger station. About a half mile past Valyermo an intersection sign will direct you to Big Pines. As you make the turn towards the wooded area you will be leaving the desert region.

Devil's Punchbowl County Park, a desert spectacular of unusual rock formations, is 2.5 miles south of this point, but as you turn uphill thoughts and sights of the desert will gradually disappear. The big pines loom ahead and you will pass the mile high sign. Campers, campsites and recreational areas soon become evident.

This is the Big Pines Recreation Area. There are units open year around for those who want to enjoy the pines overnight. At the top of the hill is Big Pines. There is a lodge type structure here and it's a pleasant spot for a breather.

From Big Pines the ride to Wrightwood is downhill through scenic countryside. At Wrightwood, a popular winter recreation area, there are adequate restaurants that cater to all tastes, including those of hungry cyclists, in case you're ready for lunch and a rest.

From Wrightwood it is a mild downhill ride to Mountain Top Junction, elevation 4,802. Here you make a northwest swing onto State 138 for a gradual downhill run over high desert. Cactus, sagebrush and sand have now replaced the tall pines. About seven and a half miles down the highway lies the Mescal Wildlife Sanctuary, a possible point of interest. You soon cross the California Aqueduct.

On the route back to Littlerock you will pass through the small town of Llano. It may not be evident now, but settlers once paid $500 to live in what was then called Llano del Rio. Job Harriman, in 1914, formed a utopian colony here. Many people paid the $500 and by 1917 two thousand acres were under cultivation.

The colony was producing ninety per cent of its food and the women exported handicraft items. Unfortunately internal problems, lack of water and mismanagement forced the

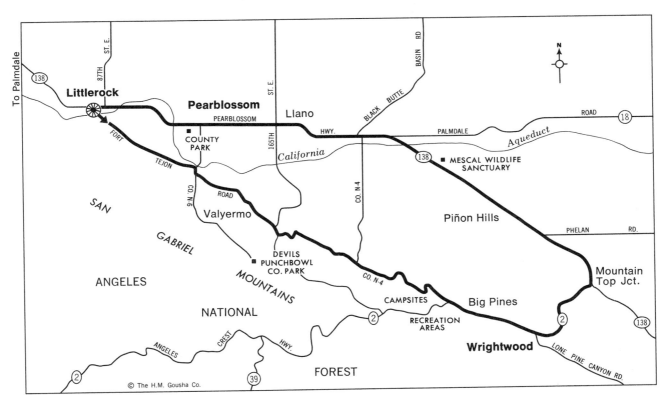

© The H.M. Gousha Co.

closing of the colony in 1918. As you ride out of Llano thoughts of utopia will be replaced by the beauty of nature in Pearblossom, the garden spot of the desert and the last town before Littlerock.

When the desert winds are blowing from the west, this return leg of the route, though mostly downhill, can be challenging. Traffic is very light throughout the loop with the exception of the Pearblossom highway, where it is moderate but not troublesome. For the experienced and capable rider this is a superb ride.

Conifer Country Adventure

Approx. mileage: 67

Rating: A

Terrain: Well-paved mountain roads.

Best times for touring: Excellent ride for spring, fall or warm winter days. The traffic is not heavy and the roads are good.

The crooked climb up from Valle Vista into the conifer country takes you past an Indian reservation, turkey farms, and an arts foundation. After the climb, the downhill return sprint provides an eerie view of planes from Banning airport flying at levels below you.

A good place to start this challenging 67-mile tour of the mountain country is Valle Vista. Travel U.S. 395 south to State 74 just below Perris. Drive east through Hemet to Valle Vista.

The small country store will provide necessary snacks for the trip. Also, you should fill water bottles before you start as the supply is limited along this route.

Heading east from Valle Vista you will ride past the Soboba Indian Reservation. The 5,000 acres, mostly grazing land, is home to less than a hundred families. The gradual uphill climb starts here, past a scattering of turkey farms, stands of willow and cottonwood, and the Cranston Ranger Station.

For a while the highway winds along the south fork of the San Jacinto River. You will begin to notice some conifers as the road gradually climbs off to the north toward Mountain Center.

This is a well-paved road built with the family car in mind. Therefore, the grades are not excessive. The uphill trip will provide breathtaking views of the mountains and the lower areas to north and east.

At Mountain Center you will turn left at the fork and continue up through a beautiful forest to Idyllwild—a recommended spot the year around. This is a resort community with a branch of the University of Southern California, the Idyllwild Arts Foundation.

Now you will slice through the high country on a good highway with the forest on both sides of you. Good turnouts for viewing are provided and you can relax by the road while you look far out across the mountains into the San Jacinto Valley.

At Lake Fulmor traces of the Indian past have been found in mortar holes in the huge boulders fringing the lake. You can picnic here, and fish, any time of the year. But camping is not permitted.

As you work your way down from the higher elevations the pines are fewer and the chaparral thicker. The downhill into Banning is a classic—the town and its airport are spread out below you. Here you may get a glimpse of the top of a plane in flight at a level below you.

From Banning you will ride along Sixth Street to Beaumont. Then follow the good Lamb Canyon Road (State 79) through the hills to San Jacinto Valley. From there it is an easy, winding ride among the foothills back to Valle Vista.

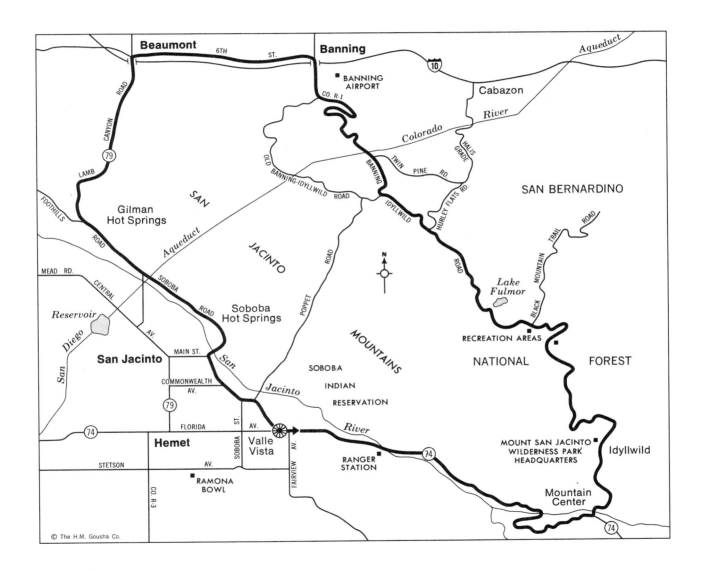

Beaumont

Banning

6TH ST.

BANNING AIRPORT

CO. R-1

10

Cabazon

Aqueduct

CANYON ROAD

79

LAMB

FOOTHILLS

ROAD

Gilman Hot Springs

SAN

JACINTO

Aqueduct

SOBOBA

ROAD

Soboba Hot Springs

OLD BANNING-IDYLLWILD ROAD

BANNING

Colorado River

TWIN PINE RD.

HALIS GRADE

HURLEY FLATS RD.

IDYLLWILD

ROAD

SAN BERNARDINO

MOUNTAIN TRAIL ROAD

BLACK

Lake Fulmor

POPPET ROAD

MOUNTAINS

SOBOBA INDIAN RESERVATION

RECREATION AREAS

NATIONAL   FOREST

MEAD RD.

CENTRAL

Reservoir

San Diego

MAIN ST.

San Jacinto

COMMONWEALTH AV.

79

74

FLORIDA

Hemet

STETSON

CO. R-3

AV.

RAMONA BOWL

SOBOBA ST.

Valle Vista

FAIRVIEW AV.

San Jacinto River

RANGER STATION

74

MOUNT SAN JACINTO WILDERNESS PARK HEADQUARTERS

Idyllwild

Mountain Center

74

© The H.M. Gousha Co.

N

Palm Springs Desert Loop

Approx. mileage: 39

Rating: B

Terrain: Flat roads through the desert agricultural area and past the well-known recreation sections.

Best times for touring: Avoid mid-summer as the heat is stupefying.

Here is an excellent 39-mile family ride in the beautiful Palm Springs area and down to Indian Wells. An excellent base ride, it is possible to extend the tour farther to Indio, Coachella and even to the Salton Sea, if you wish.

Palm Springs City Hall is a good starting place. So is Ruth Hardy Park in the center of town where there is adequate parking. From here you leave town and head out into the beautiful desert area in the vicinity of Thousand Palms. Just to the east can be seen Indio Hills. The importance of agriculture

here becomes very apparent as you ride through the irrigated desert that water has turned into a huge year-round garden. The growing season exceeds 280 days a year and rainfall is under four inches.

Ride down Varner Road and Washington Street through Indian Wells, laced with many irrigation canals from the deep wells. Cottonwoods and the ornamental, feathery tamarisks grow in this area. Golf courses abound.

A good place to stop and relax is Palm Desert. You pass a shopping center where you can have lunch. After you eat, ride up Bob Hope Drive past more exclusive golf clubs.

Along Date Palm Drive you pass roadside fruit stands that specialize in dates. By all means stop and buy. You will be amazed at the many different kinds. The date palm gardens line the roads in this area. Stop a while and relax while you are amongst these unique trees—this

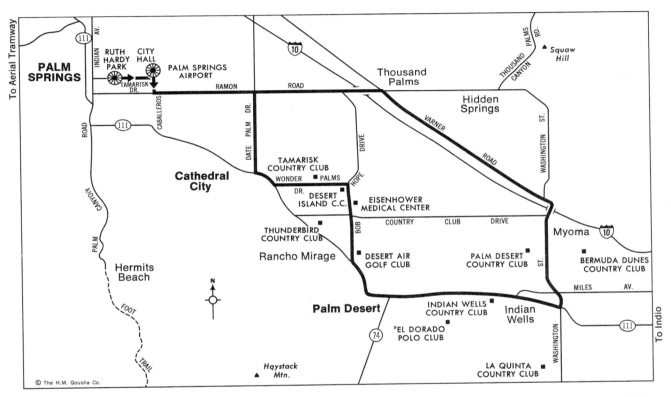

is one of the few places in the world where dates are grown.

The route soon takes you back to Palm Springs. Tour the town and enjoy this posh desert community with the stark, beautiful mountains in the background. At 135 E. Tahquitz-McCallum Way is the Palm Springs Desert Museum, which is open from September to June with natural history and art exhibits.

A few miles north of Palm Springs is the world's longest single span aerial tramway. In a few minutes you ascend from the desert floor to the 8,516-foot station on Mt. San Jacinto. There is picnicking and camping and a cafe. Last car to the top leaves at 6:30 p.m.

The Cool Century—A Hundred Miles of Surf

Approx. mileage: 100

Rating: A

Terrain: The route follows the coast highway. There are some hills but the road is mostly flat.

Best times for touring: An excellent tour anytime, but most pleasant during the warmer seasons. Some heavy traffic.

If you like salt breezes you'll like this cool Pacific coast tour —one of the best "century" runs in California. The route takes you from the Santa Monica area, 50 miles up the shoreline to Oxnard, past beautiful beaches, and back. And, of course, all along the way are the fringe benefits—watching the surfers skillfully maneuver their surfboards and the girls their bikinis.

A good starting place is Brentwood at San Vicente and Bundy. Past the Brentwood Country Club nip down through the Santa Monica Canyon to Pacific Coast Highway (State 1).

Almost immediately you hit Will Rogers State Beach. The State Park, also named after the country humorist, is four miles inland. The Rogers family donated 186 acres to California in 1944. On the land, buildings and grounds are maintained as they were prior to Rogers' death.

Watch for Pacific Palisades and its cliffside homes and Topanga Canyon Road that spews hot valley dwellers onto the cool beaches. In succession come Las Tunas, La Costa, and Carbon beaches before you reach Malibu—world famous center of surfing action.

Malibu has a lot to recommend it—great swimming beaches, good fishing, clusters of attractive homes. Call a rest stop at Malibu Pier to watch the wiggly fish and girls awhile before striking out again.

Leaving the shoreline a few miles you bypass Pt. Dume and drop back again at Zuma Beach, one of the most popular in Los Angeles County. It has two miles of ocean frontage, lifeguards and restrooms.

Just up the coast is Leo Carrillo State Beach spreading out on both sides of the highway. Named for the movie actor—and park commissioner— the beach strip has been a star in its own right as the location of many early movies.

After Point Mugu State Park you soon leave the ocean and pedal alongside the Pacific Missile Range. In about a mile you should take a right exit at Las Posas Road. Then ride left and cross over the freeway, traveling north past the main gate of the Missile Range and alongside a golf course.

At Hueneme Road turn left. Ride to the right on Perkins, then jog along left a short way on Pleasant Valley Road. A right hook on J Street takes you to Bubbling Springs Park.

Bubbling Springs is a dandy spot for a sack snack, if you brought one. If not, there are good restaurants in Oxnard, site of the Naval Construction Battalion Center (these are the fellows famous for "The impossible takes a little longer"). Follow the

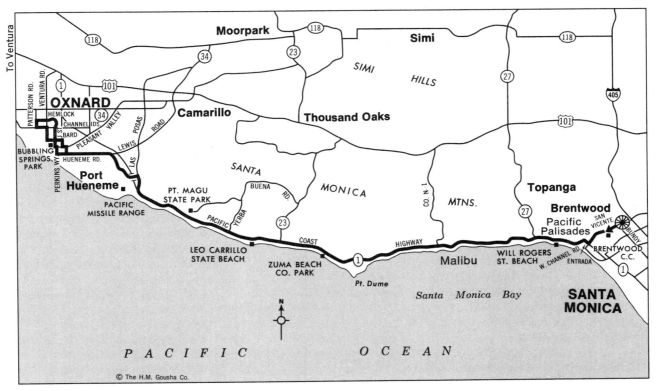

© The H.M. Gousha Co.

route via J Street, Guava to Patterson. Turn east on Channel Islands Blvd., down Ventura to Bard. At the high school make a right on C Street. Pick up Pleasant Valley and then Cypress to get back to Hueneme Road, the way you came in.

Usually on the return junket down the coast you are assisted by an excellent tailwind. Another assist is a foxy dodge around the Malibu hill. About halfway up the slope is a one-way entry street leading onto the Coast Highway. Dismount, walk around the barrier. After 15 or 20 feet remount and follow the beach level road down past the oceanside homes.

You reenter the highway at Malibu. From there on it is a clear shot down the coast and up the road to your starting place and the end of the cool century run.

San Diego Area

(Selected by Dr. Clifford L. Graves)

San Diego Loop to La Jolla

Approx. mileage: 30

Rating: C

Terrain: Mostly flat, if you stay on the designated route and skirt the hills in La Jolla.

Best times for touring: Equally good, winter and summer. City traffic can be a hazard, particularly near Sea World and in the downtown area of La Jolla.

Start at Sea World. Ride east on Sea World Drive and north on East Mission Bay Drive until you come to Fiesta Island. Circumnavigate the island, then return to East Mission Bay Drive and continue north. At De Anza Cove, circle the golf course till you come to Grand Avenue. Heavy traffic here, but you can escape it quickly by switching to Thomas Avenue as soon as you have passed the high school. Continue west till you come to Bayard; then turn north.

When you arrive at Turquoise Street at the northern limit of Pacific Beach, you have a choice. The main route marked on the map stays close to the ocean and avoids any steep hills. If you want more exercise, take La Jolla Hermosa Avenue Drive up into the Muirlands—you have a good climb for a few miles. Nautilus Street takes you back to sea level.

Continue on Nautilus till it ends at the ocean, then wind your way north to La Jolla Cove. This is a good place for a picnic.

You will now be in heavy traffic for about a mile as you follow Prospect Street away from the Cove and pick up Torrey Pines Road. At La Jolla Shores Drive turn left and make for Kellogg Park, which is another good place for a picnic. The aquarium at Scripps Institution of Oceanography is worth a stop.

Up the hill is the campus of the University of California. See the quad at Revelle College, ringed by splendid buildings and graced by an ornamental fountain. If you have time, cross the footbridge to the Matthews campus with the medical school and the veterans hospital. Another impressive building is the central library which rises implausibly like a giant mushroom from a grove of eucalyptus trees.

Return to La Jolla by way of Torrey Pines Road. Girard Avenue has many fancy shops and is fine for window shopping. Ride south over the same route you saw before until you come to Turquoise again. Here you do a bit of zigzagging on side streets—stay as close to the ocean as possible. You pass the Crystal Fishing Pier and reach the northern limit of Mission Beach, an interesting spit of land three miles long and a few hundred yards across. On the ocean side it has what amounts to a board walk where you can ride your bike undisturbed by cars. On the bay side, it has a sidewalk between the homes and the beach. This too can be ridden by bike if you stay single file and watch out for cats and dogs.

Your road back to Sea World leads across the Ventura Bridge on a road called West Mission Bay Drive. As soon as you have crossed the bridge, turn right and you will see the Islandia Hotel. It faces Quivira Basin which you can circumnavigate almost entirely. Where the Islandia Hotel faces the basin is a landing dock and snackbar, good for a rest.

To get back to Sea World takes a bit of doing, since most of the space is taken up by a giant intersection for cars. It is possible to avoid this speedway if you will go back to the traffic light on West Mission Bay Drive, just south of the Ventura Bridge. Cross West Mission Bay Drive and you find yourself at Perez Cove. Here, another traffic light guides you across the causeway with its endless streams of cars. Sea World is directly ahead.

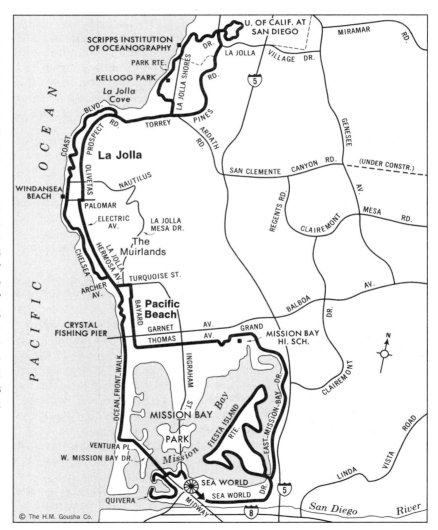

History Highlights in San Diego

Approx. mileage: 30

Rating: C

Terrain: Mostly flat, with maximum elevation of 500 feet.

Best times for touring: Equally good, winter or summer. City traffic is always a hazard, but not especially serious except at a few key intersections.

Pepper Grove in Balboa Park is a convenient starting point. Ride west on Laurel till you come to First Avenue, then north to Washington. Turn left and watch for signs near the corner of Goldfinch and Lewis. Follow the signs to Presidio Park, a fine vantage point.

Going down the hill on Presidio Drive, you pass Fort Stockton on the left and the Serra Museum on the right. Stop here a while. The famous Mormon Battalion billeted at Fort Stockton in 1847. It has one of the two guns that were used in the defense of the town in 1846. The Serra Museum gives a fine view over Mission Valley and Point Loma. Halfway down the slope towards Old Town, you will see excavations. This is the site of the Spanish presidio which functioned here from 1769 to the 1820's.

When you get to the bottom of the hill, turn left on Taylor, go a few blocks, and turn left on San Diego Avenue, which is the access road to Old Town Plaza, a historic spot. The flagpole stands where a Lt. Rowan raised the American flag on July 29, 1846, without Mexican opposition.

Spend a few minutes on the Plaza. It has many old and partly restored buildings. The whole area is a state historical monument. The Estudillo house on the southeast corner (often erroneously called Ramona's marriage place) is well worth a visit. It dates from the 1820's.

Now retrace your route as far as Taylor Street, turn left, cross San Diego Freeway, and continue west till you are in the Ocean Beach area. Sunset Cliffs is a dramatic escarpment with perpendicular dropoffs to the pounding surf. You now make a stiff climb up Hill Street to gain the spine of the Point Loma peninsula. It might be best to walk it.

Make a right on Catalina Boulevard and continue south as far as the road goes. It takes you to Cabrillo National Monument with an expansive view of the harbor and the coast. The grey whales migrate along the coast from the middle of December till the middle of March, and they are easily visible from Point Loma. If you have taken a sandwich, sit down and have a picnic.

Complete the circle by retracing your steps as far as Catalina Boulevard, then Canon Street. Make the Shelter Island loop, then take North Harbor Drive back to the city. If you have time, visit Harbor Island. Laurel Street is the best route back to Balboa Park. Walk it.

For the northern extension of this San Diego Highlights tour, see pages 58 and 59.

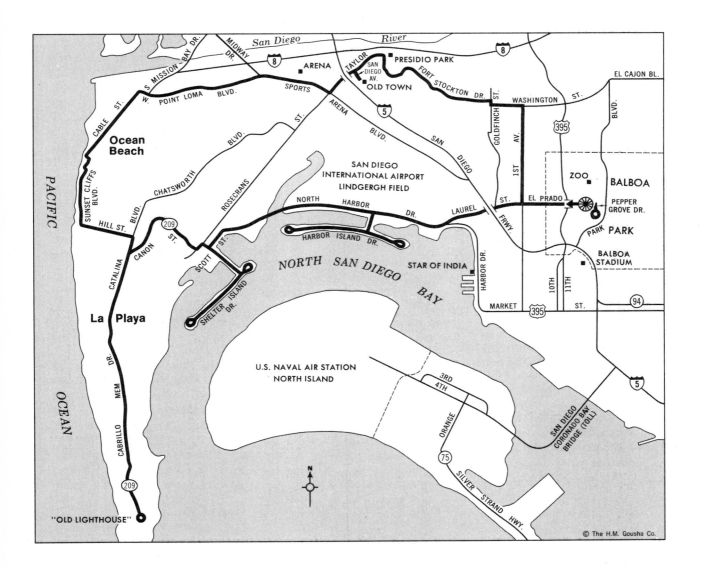

61

Beach Ride to Oceanside

Approx. mileage: 50

Rating: B

Terrain: Gentle grades, good roads with wide shoulders.

Best times for touring: Equally good in winter and summer; it can be foggy in spring, but not enough to interfere with cycling.

One of the most enjoyable bicycle tours in the San Diego area is the coast road north. Relieved of heavy traffic by the nearby freeway, it is favored with wide shoulders, gentle grades and fair winds.

This is a good test ride for the beginner because there are several options. From the campus of the University of California in La Jolla to Oceanside and back on the same road is a comfortable 50 miles. But if that sounds too strenuous, you can turn around at Encinitas and cut the distance in half.

On the other hand, if you're an eager beaver and want to get the most out of the ride, you can run up to Oceanside along the coast and then cut inland about five miles and ride south over El Camino Real (so called because it was the route of the Spanish soldiers on their trek to Monterey in 1769). Between Encinitas and Oceanside, this is identified as S-11. South of Encinitas, it is less well defined but still fairly easy to follow.

A 50-mile ride might normally get an "A" rating, but this one is only a "B" because of the many assists you get along the way. Most important is the wind. In the morning it blows from the southwest, giving you a boost as you pedal north from La Jolla. In the afternoon, it blows from the northwest so you get a tailwind again. The wide shoulders and gentle grades of the coast highway are another big assist. And eating places are numerous. Or you take a lunch and have a picnic at the beach at any one of the numerous parks.

This trip can be made into a fine overnight camping trip if you like to dawdle along the way and spend as much time sunning on the sand as you do on the bike. Camping is allowed at both South Carlsbad Beach State Park and San Elijo State Beach.

Your first chance to sightsee comes right at the start on the campus of the University of California. Spend a little time riding around if you've not seen the area before. The main library is especially interesting.

Six miles north of the campus is Del Mar; in the summer, this is famous for its state fair and horse racing.

Near Encinitas, you come to vast fields of flowers under cultivation; in the spring, this is a riot of color. For a close look, switch inland on Highway S-9 (San Marcos), then take S-11 north. You can get back to the coast at Batiquitos Lagoon. The Buena Vista Lagoon between Carlsbad and Oceanside is a bird sanctuary.

On the way home, you can have a marvelous ride on the beach *if* the tide is going out. From Torrey Pines State Park south, you can pedal down a deserted beach with only the sandpipers and seagulls for company. On your left, the cliffs reach up for hundreds of feet. At one point, you have to shoulder your bike and negotiate a short catwalk over a cliff.

After about three miles, you come to a spot where you can leave the beach over a steep road going up the cliffside. It is about half a mile north of the Scripps pier, which is easily identifiable. This cliff road puts you on La Jolla Farms Road, less than a mile from the U. C. campus.

Tour extension for those tempted to extend the ride. North of Oceanside, you run into Interstate 5 freeway which is off limits to bicyclists. However, there is a parallel road on Camp Pendleton which will take you all the way to San Clemente. Always obtain prior permission to cross Camp Pendleton. Write to the Provost Marshal, Camp Pendleton 92055 at least two weeks before you expect to make the trip.

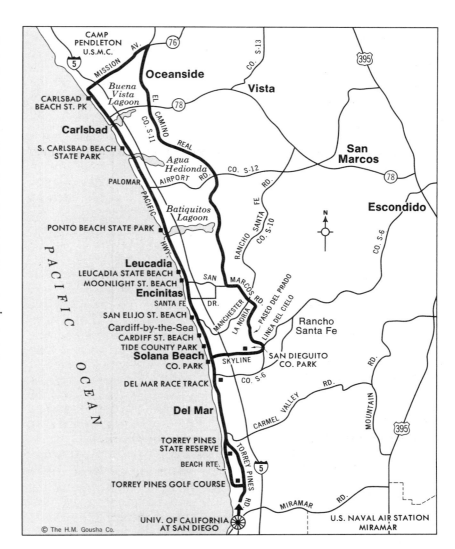

Rancho Santa Fe—Cyclist's Paradise

Approx. mileage: 18

Rating: C

Terrain: Many hills with very little flat land in between. However, the grades are short.

Best times for touring: Anytime of the year.

Four miles inland from Solana Beach is an area of luxurious homes and beautiful estates called Rancho Santa Fe. It measures about four miles in each direction, and is one of the loveliest spots in all of southern California.

Not only is it great for residents, but also for visiting cyclists who can spend some very pleasant hours winding their way through the area, looking at the homes, the orange groves, and the beautiful views.

The pleasure is all in the cycling. No famous tourist at-

tractions here. Just the wonderful peace of mind. If you can't get along without an occasional stop, Rancho Santa Fe does have a golf course, a duck pond and a very charming shopping district. For shade, there are many stands of eucalyptus. If you grow hungry, there are two restaurants and a market in what might be called downtown.

If this route is too limited and you want more exercise, use the University of California in La Jolla as your start-stop point. By doing so, you add about 20 miles to the 18 within Rancho Santa Fe itself, and add enough difficulty to make the longer route worthy of a B rating.

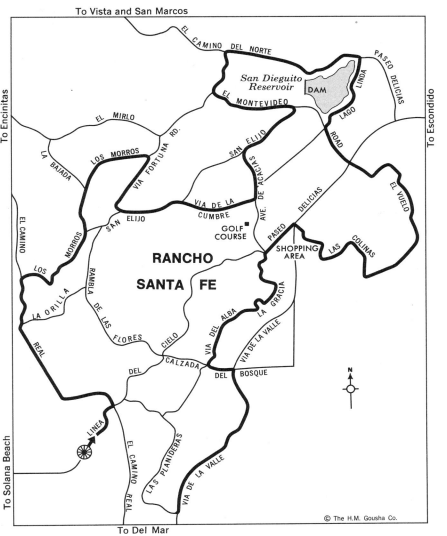

To Vista and San Marcos

To Encinitas

To Escondido

EL CAMINO DEL NORTE

San Dieguito Reservoir

DAM

PASEO DELICIAS

LINDA

EL MONTEVIDEO

EL MIRLO

LAGO

ROAD

VIA FORTUNA RD.

SAN ELIJO

LA BAJADA

LOS MORROS

AVE. DE ACACIAS

EL VUELO

VIA DE LA CUMBRE

PASEO DELICIAS

EL CAMINO

SAN

ELIJO

GOLF COURSE

LAS COLINAS

RANCHO

SHOPPING AREA

LOS

SANTA FE

MORROS

RAMBLA DE LAS FLORES

LA ORILLA

LA GRACIA

VIA DEL ALBA

VIA DE LA VALLE

REAL

CIELO

CALZADA

DEL

DEL BOSQUE

N

LINEA

EL CAMINO REAL

LAS PLANIDERAS

VIA DE LA VALLE

To Solana Beach

To Del Mar

© The H.M. Gousha Co.

65

Through Avocado Orchards to Pala

Approx. mileage: 24 (40 miles if you take the Pala Mission loop.)

Rating: C

Terrain: Plenty of ups and downs through hilly country, but no severe climbs.

Best times for touring: This ride is hot in summer but there are shady spots along the way and the traffic is heavy only in a few freeway stretches.

This tour has the kind of roads dear to a bicyclist. There are little roads that twist and turn, rise and dip from the starting point at Bonsall through avocado groves and a tunnel of live oaks, cross well-tilled fields and look our over a constantly shifting panorama.

You also have a chance for a double loop trip—a ride to Pala Mission in Indian country and an extra trip to Rancho California, in the Temecula Valley.

To start, drive to Bonsall, a crossroads on the San Luis Rey River 12 miles inland from Oceanside on State Highway 76. Out of Bonsall ride north on Olive Hill Road, that rises abruptly and winds back and forth, until you come to a small reservoir. Here, turn left and enjoy cruising along in the peace and quiet until you eventually reach S-13 (Mission Road), where there is a stop sign.

Ride south for a little over a mile, then turn left on Live Oak Park Road. The next three miles are lovely countryside studded with avocado groves. At the T-junction with Reche Road, where there is a stop sign, turn right. In another mile you are at pleasant Live Oak Country Park where you may spread out your picnic in the shade.

After lunch retrace for half a mile and, turning right, follow Live Oak Park Road through a magnificent stand of live oaks that make a shady tunnel of the road for more than a mile. At the next stop sign, you reach East Mission Road. Turn right and coast down to State 395.

(This is the time to decide whether or not to take the loop trip up Rainbow Canyon and over to Pala Mission.)

For the short trip, turn right onto U.S. 395. The highway is not freeway here but the traffic is heavy for the mile you will travel it. Then turn right again on Reche Road which takes you back to Live Oak Park. From here, head south over Gird Road past the Fallbrook Golf Course to State Highway 76. In a few more miles, the short loop is complete and you are back in Bonsall.

This same ride can be lengthened to 40 miles if you head north on State 395 when you first reach it. In less than a mile, pick up the old road that parallels the new. Now east of the highway, you soon see the small community of Rainbow. Continue north on Rainbow Canyon Road to the intersection of U.S. 395 and State 71-79. Here, at the edge of Rancho California is a beautiful view of the Temecula Valley.

You may be interested in a secondary loop trip to the rather classy Rancho California shopping center a few miles north. There is a restaurant and snack bar that are open only on weekends.

The road back is through Pechanga Indian country. Highway S-16 takes you to Pala and the mission that is over 150 years old. It is well preserved—one of the few working missions. After Pala, turn west on State 76. The road snakes along an escarpment above the San Luis River and the views you get at sunset are spectacular.

Cross U.S. 395 and continue on State 76 back to the starting place at Bonsall.

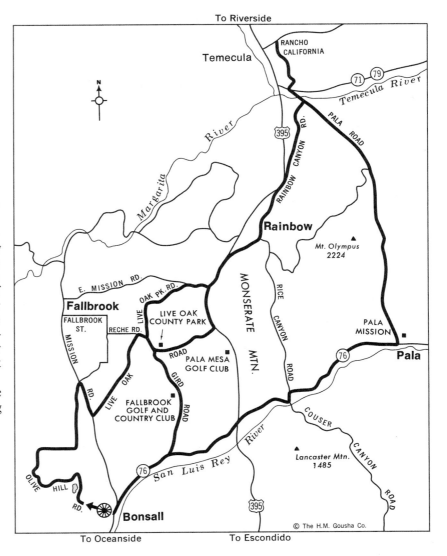

Bikeway to the Stars

Approx. mileage: 53 (31 without Palomar loop)

Rating: A

Terrain: Steep, circuitous roads through mountain country.

Best times for touring: Especially beautiful in autumn. Use extreme care, particularly on Sundays, because the traffic is often heavy.

The best known route to the top of Mt. Palomar, if you are driving, is the Highway to the Stars (S6, the road up from Escondido). However, for the bicyclist, a better route to Palomar Observatory is S7, the East Grade Road that starts at Lake Henshaw. The climb is much more gradual and there is less traffic. You might even decide to camp on the mountain, saving the twisty S6 for the downhill ride back the next day.

Lake Henshaw on State 76 provides outstanding fishing—crappie, bluegill, bass and catfish. Accommodations include campground, cabins, trailer park. There is also a restaurant and a store. Provisions are slim along the route ahead so stock up on snacks.

Past Lake Henshaw one mile northwest you will see S7 on your right. Don't miss it because if you do, you will have to climb the mountain over the steep Highway to the Stars.

Rising gradually through a wooded region with occasional clearings, this route is especially impressive in autumn when the black oaks are showing color. You should not have to walk any part—just gear down.

Eventually, after an 11-mile, two-and-a-half hour climb, you come to the intersection with the Highway to the Stars. Take a rest here and make up your mind about the rest of the ride. If you head down the mountain, your circuit will be 31 miles. But you can extend your route by taking a loop visit to the observatory—another 22 miles.

The great silver dome housing the Hale celestial telescope, the world's largest, dominates the summit. From 8:30 a.m. to 5:30 p.m. each day from the glass-enclosed gallery you may view the massive telescope with the 200-inch mirror. Three other domes with smaller instruments and a museum are also on the mountain.

Just outside the observatory grounds is a picnic area. At nearby Crestline is a store that will furnish information about the many campgrounds in the area, in case you have decided to make this a two-day junket.

Your descent from Palomar down S6 to State 76 is a 6.7-mile schuss with 50 switchbacks. The angled road gives you even more spectacular overviews than the route up from Lake Henshaw. But be careful while admiring the scenery. The traffic can be very heavy, especially on Sunday.

When you reach Highway 67 make a left turn to return to Lake Henshaw. The route will follow the San Luis Rey River part of the way and will also pass through sections of the La Jolla Indian Reservation.

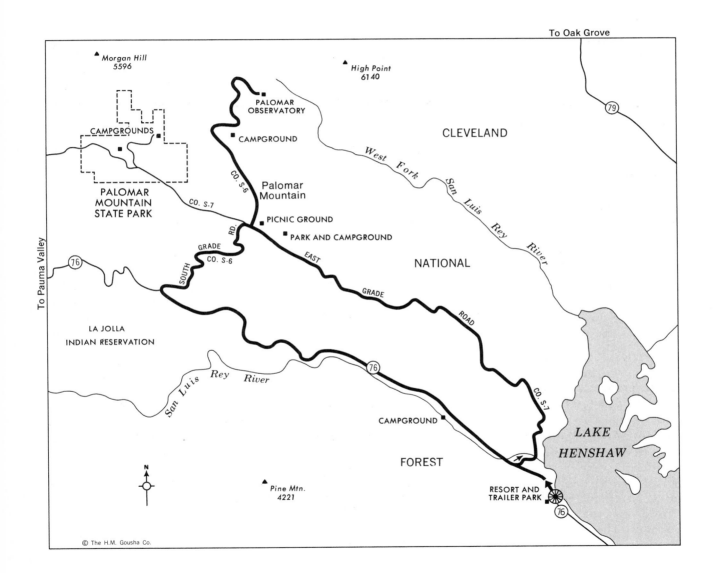

To Oak Grove

Morgan Hill
5596

High Point
6140

79

CLEVELAND

PALOMAR
OBSERVATORY

CAMPGROUND

CAMPGROUNDS

West Fork

San Luis Rey River

PALOMAR
MOUNTAIN
STATE PARK

CO. S-6

Palomar
Mountain

CO. S-7

PICNIC GROUND

PARK AND CAMPGROUND

NATIONAL

To Pauma Valley

RD.

GRADE

76

SOUTH

CO. S-6

EAST

GRADE

ROAD

LA JOLLA
INDIAN RESERVATION

San Luis Rey River

76

CO. S-7

LAKE
HENSHAW

N

Pine Mtn.
4221

CAMPGROUND

FOREST

RESORT AND
TRAILER PARK

76

© The H.M. Gousha Co.

Gentlemen's Ride—Escondido to San Luis Rey

Approx. mileage: 50

Rating: A

Terrain: Fairly easy going, but the first eight miles are tricky—many twists and turns.

Best times for touring: All year.

This circuit starts in Felicita Park near Escondido and then leads clockwise toward Vista, then Bonsall, Lilac, Valley Center and back to the starting point. Locally, it is known as the "gentleman's ride" after the Grand Prix des Gentlemen in France.

The roads are quiet, and the scenery is lovely. Of particular appeal is the great variety of the countryside. After leaving Escondido, you enter a residential-farming district. Then, on Richland Road, the scene shifts to turkey ranches. In Twin Oaks, you are back on the farm.

Foothill Drive affords a view of a rapidly vanishing southern California scene—orange groves. Gopher Canyon, on the approach to the valley of San Luis Rey, has many fine horse ranches. The golf course in the valley supplies a touch of the

twentieth century. (At the golf course, take care not to cross the river; this route stays on the south side.)

Beyond this point, you enter gradually rising country that is as yet untouched. As you reach the higher elevations, the views become more impressive. When the weather is clear, both Mount Palomar and Mount San Gorgonio are easily visible. The countryside gets very rugged at Lilac. East of the freeway, Lilac Road turns to dirt—but not for long. At Valley Center, you are back in civilization.

Felicita Park makes an ideal start-stop point. It has a large picnic area among the oak trees, with tables, fireplaces and restrooms.

Places to eat along the route are few and far between. Bonsall and Valley Center have markets, but it's slim pickings in other settlements. Take a sandwich, and avoid the problem.

Escondido offers plenty of restaurants and accommodations if you want to stay overnight for another day of cycling. Ferrara Winery on West 15th Street is open daily for those who like to sample the local product.

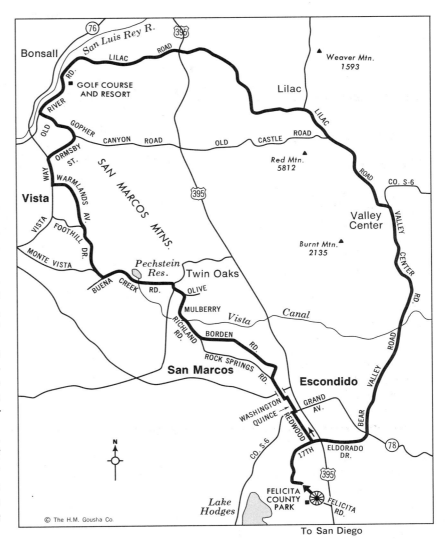

© The H.M. Gousha Co.

A Safari to San Pasqual

Approx. mileage: 40

Rating: B

Terrain: Gentle hills for the most part; Pasqual Grade is challenging.

Best times for touring: All year.

The best starting point for this ride through history is Rancho Bernardo. Make it in a clockwise direction to take advantage of the west wind on the climb up Pasqual Grade.

There are plenty of opportunities to stop and eat. There is one restaurant at San Pasqual and a handful in Ramona. For a picnic, the best spot is the San Pasqual Battlefield State Historic Monument.

From Rancho Bernardo, take Pomerado Road north till you get to Lake Hodges. Then turn left and climb onto the freeway (U.S. 395). This is an unusual piece of freeway, in that bicyclists are allowed because there are no alternate routes. The prospect may sound scary, but you're actually on the freeway for less than a mile and you should have no troubles.

As soon as you have crossed the Lake Hodges bridge, take the off-ramp. After a bit of winding, you find yourself on the San Pasqual Road, which takes you to State Route 78 and the battle monument. Pause here for awhile, and recall the details of the historic battle.

It was early on the morning of December 6, 1846, that General Stephen Kearney led his bone weary dragoons down the trail (still visible east of the road) and into battle with a well-armed Mexican force under Andres Pico. Kearney and his tired band of 100 had been on the road for months, hauling supplies and two 800-pound howitzers across the endless Gila Trail into Yuma and then to Pasqual.

The Mexicans knew an attack was coming, and Pico deployed his 150 men at the foot of the trail about a mile east of the monument. Kearney thought the mere sight of his men would send the Mexicans running. But the advantage was all with the Mexicans, who had fresh horses, strong lances and dry powder to set against the tired Americans who tried to attack with muskets that would not fire.

Kearney attacked as soon as possible, but his men were picked off one by one. Nine died on the first charge. The Mexicans then wheeled and retreated to the spot where the monument now stands. The Americans chased and were engaged in hand-to-hand combat. Another 11 died, and a total of 18 more were injured, including General Kearney. After a three-day siege at Mule Hill (near the spot where you crossed Lake Hodges on the freeway), the Americans were freed by an expeditionary force sent out from San Diego.

The battle was fought in vain. Unknown to the combatants, San Diego had already passed

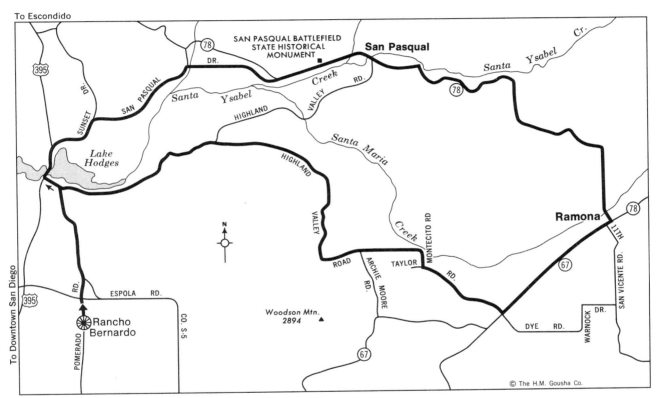

back into American hands and there was no need for any more struggle.

After your exploration of the monument, continue your ride up the San Pasqual Grade into Ramona. (You pass the Wild Animal Park but you probably won't have the time for a visit.) A good rest point in Ramona is Collier County Park—shade trees, picnic tables and rest rooms.

From there, take Highway 67 southwest for three and a half miles and pick up Highland Valley Road which takes you back to Lake Hodges.

Rugged Ride into Japatul Valley

Approx. mileage: 40

Rating: A

Terrain: Rugged mountains, with very stiff climbs along the route.

Best times for touring: All year, except very hot and very cold days.

This loop takes you into some of San Diego County's most remote back country. You're free of traffic and commercial developments, and you can ride for miles in peaceful splendor. But there's a price to pay for all this wonderful quiet and spectacular views. The riding is tough. Total mileage is only 40, but by the end of the day you may think you've gone a hundred because of the strain of those uphill grinds.

You'll also be without service facilities or restaurants. But if you have normal tools and a lunch with you, this handicap is easily overcome.

A convenient starting point is the Singing Hills Country Club at the corner of Dehesa Road and Willow Glen Drive, two miles east of El Cajon. The loop can be taken either clockwise or counterclockwise.

If you go clockwise, you face some long grades on the outward leg. They'll come easier if you concentrate on your immediate surroundings rather than the far off summits that look so high and so distant. Find the gear that you can comfortably handle and establish a cadence. Slowly but surely, you'll make it, and the exercise can be very relaxing.

If you find yourself running completely out of steam, you can cut the ride short by switching off for Alpine after you've gone about seven miles from the starting point. The grades are severe at this point, and the whole idea may lose its appeal if you face exhaustion this close to the start of the ride.

Roads generally are good; there are a few miles of dirt at Japatul. After you leave Japatul on the return leg, you take Lyons Valley Road past the Japatul Forest Station, and then

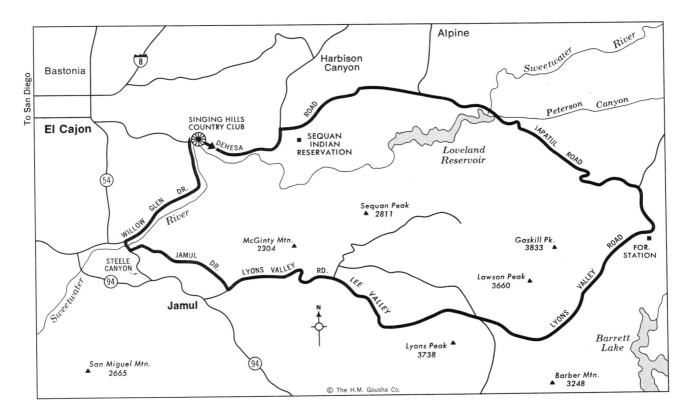

turn west between Lawson Peak and Lyons Peak to Lee Valley Road which will take you into Jamul. However, because of heavy traffic on Highway 94, it is best to cut off on Jamul Drive one mile before reaching Jamul. Ride to Sweet- water River and turn left on Steel Canyon Road. This will take you to Willow Glen Drive at the Cottonwood Country Club; from there it is only a few miles back to your starting point.

You're likely not to see a house or other sign of human habitation along this circuit except on Willow Glen Road. The hillsides are shrub-covered all the way until you enter some lovely live oak stands close to Lyons Peak.

The Borrego Springs Challenge

Approx. mileage: 50

Rating: A

Terrain: Difficult grades and very dry desert country. This one is reserved for strong riders who can finish what they start. This circuit has no shortcuts; once committed, you must complete the 50 miles.

Best times for touring: Winter or spring. Summer and fall are too hot.

Borrego Springs is the only logical starting point, unless you're camping in Anza-Borrego State Park and want to return to your campsite at the end of the ride. Regardless of where you start, take the route in a clockwise direction, so you can make the most difficult climb up to 4,000 feet at Ranchita on a gradual slope, and then make a ten-mile schuss back to Borrego Springs. Counter-clockwise, the circuit confronts you with a very steep climb in the first ten miles.

This is dry and desolate country, so fill your water bottle before you leave and make meal plans in advance. The only real restaurant is in Borrego. There is a store at Ranchita and a beer bar in San Felipe, but that is all. If in doubt about your travel times, take a sandwich.

Starting at Borrego Springs, head south on Borrego Springs Road to Yaqui Pass. The scenic overlook at the top is at 1,750 feet. The road then drops down to Tamarisk Campground, one of the most popular in the state park. Northwest of the intersection of Borrego Springs Road and State 78 is Yaqui Well, an excellent place to observe birds and other wildlife native to this desert country.

Sentenac Canyon is a jumble of rocks, stones, gravel and boulders. At Scissors Crossing, turn northwest on Route S-2 to San Felipe. Your main obstacle here, besides a mild gradient, is the wind that usually blows from the northwest. This is the route of the legendary Butterfield stagecoaches that linked the desert communities in the 1850's and 1860's.

San Felipe marks the halfway point. You'd better eat something here to forestall fatigue on the last half of the trip. A few miles beyond San Felipe you turn east on S-22 for the run back to Borrego Springs.

Anza-Borrego State Park can keep you busy during any spare time you might have before or after the ride. This is a spectacular piece of desert, with many isolated spots for camping, fascinating geologic formations, and a wide range of plant and wildlife. Rangers at the park headquarters can give you ideas on touring; the nearby Palm Canyon Campground is the best of the park. Here is a rare opportunity to combine some challenging cycling with an offbeat camping adventure.

If the rigorous ride dictates a shower and soft mattress, you'll find accommodations in and around Borrego Springs. This has become a lively desert resort community over the past decade. But the real charm of this country is the wide open desert that has not yet been overrun by too many recreational vehicles.

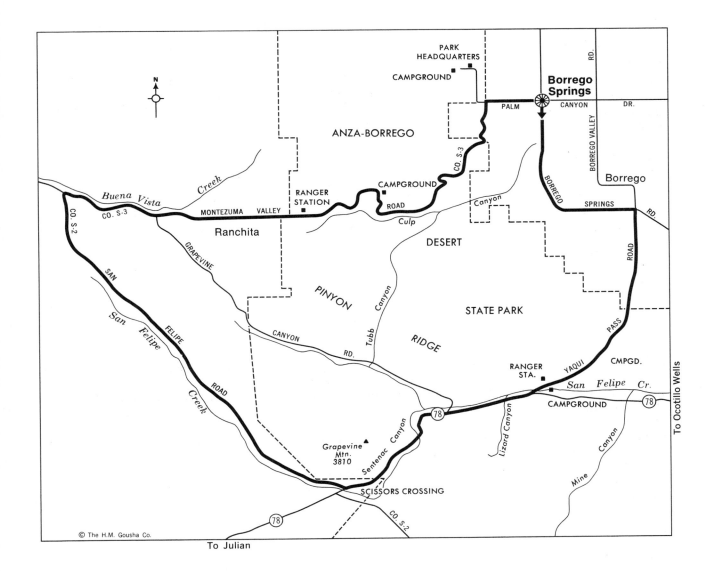

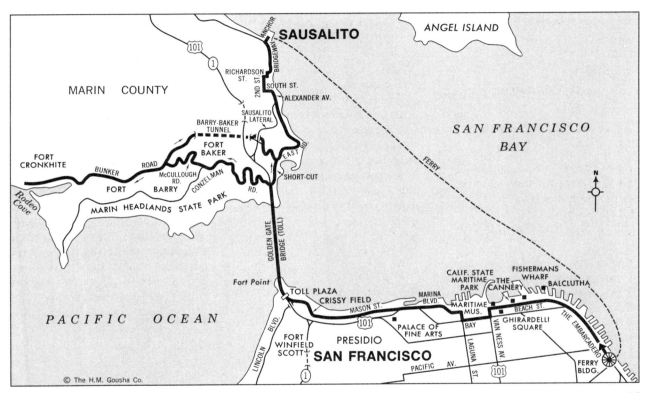

lice Station. Several days before your trip, call 561-2251 to make arrangements. On the morning of the trip confirm the hour you will need the escort. When you reach the eastern end of the tunnel continue downhill and head into Sausalito, a picturesque and crowded mecca of shops, crafts, restaurants, tourists and boats.

The ferry boat for the return trip to the city leaves from the foot of Anchor Street during the day. The schedule changes so call 982-8833 for times. Fare: adults-50 cents, under 17-25 cents, bikes-free.

To lengthen the trip to 36 miles, avoid the ferry and return via the same route. Watch the afternoon traffic from San Francisco—it is terrific.

Winding Road to Belvedere and Beyond

Approx. mileage: 20

Rating: B

Terrain: The route varies from flat to rolling hills. There are two steep grades—one long and one short.

Best times for touring: Good all year. Expect heavy traffic in Tiburon and main highways.

This short tour has just about everything—postcard views of the Bay and Tiburon Peninsula, interesting spots for lunch and browsing, and all degrees of difficulty for the bicyclist.

Your venture can begin anywhere along the route. Strawberry Shopping Center is a convenient spot. Head south, following the service road on to Seminary Drive. Strawberry Drive then takes you out to Tiburon Blvd.

Look out for traffic here. The two-lane road is loaded on the weekends. Soon, take Greenwood Road to avoid some of the cars. A nice contrast to the luxurious waterside apartments you pass is a lovely old yellow and white Victorian house, usually with a yardful of sleek seagulls. This is the National Audubon Society.

Just as you rejoin Tiburon Blvd. near Trestle Glen Blvd., in a flat stretch between the two hills, you will see a fenced-off grave, often decorated with flowers. This is the resting place for Blackie, a beloved old sway-backed horse who lived in the field for years.

Richardson Bay Park lies below as you negotiate the hill. Leave Tiburon Blvd. for San Raphael Avenue and then continue up around Belvedere on West Shore Road. The going is very tough here for a short way, so don't be ashamed to get off and walk. At the top of the grade is a tree-lined road that offers a spectacular view of Angel Island out across Raccoon Straits and Belvedere Cove with its yacht harbors. You will pass spectacular houses, some of the world's most expensive real estate.

Curving Main Street is the tourist center of Tiburon. There are several really good restaurants and a handful of unusual shops to browse through. If you bring your own lunch, try wine tasting at the Tiburon Vintners. Or buy your favorite wine and enjoy a picnic on the shore at the corner of Main and Paradise Drive.

Paradise Drive is a winding, narrow, mildly hilly, picturesque road. An ultimate in bicycling pleasure! Ride past the Tiburon Oceanographic Center and the Paradise Beach County Park. There is an excellent picnic area. If the weather is reasonable you might like to take time out for a swim.

More twisting road and spectacular views and you come to the Paradise Cove end of Trestle Glen Blvd. If you decide to cut your trip short, now is the chance. Turn onto Trestle Glen at the firehouse and head back down Tiburon Blvd. to the Strawberry Shopping Center.

To take the long way around, turn right on to San Clemente and left at Tamalpais. After you cross over U.S. 101 watch closely for Chapman Drive and turn left. It is not only a difficult street to find, it is even more difficult to follow its twisting, uphill path. Be patient and take your time in low gear. If Chapman is too hard even in low gear, try walking for a change of pace.

Be prepared for a sensational long downhill run just after Chapman joins Camino Alto. Here you can imagine yourself a racer and you won't even have to work for speed. If you have time on the downhill slope, grab a peek at the panoramic view of Richardson Bay.

East Blithedale Avenue is the home stretch that takes you back to the starting point at Strawberry Shopping Center.

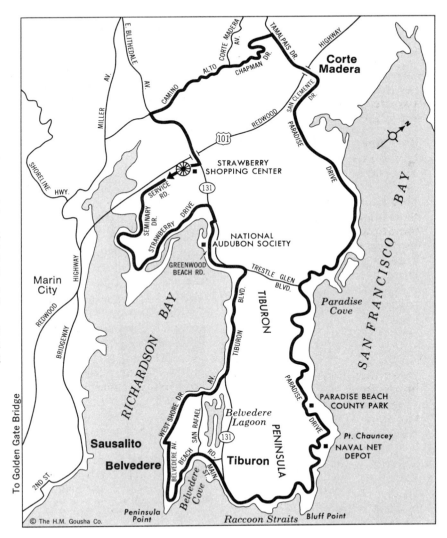

Through Rural Marin and a Redwood Park

Approx. mileage: 30

Rating: B

Terrain: Mostly flat with two major uphill climbs.

Best times for touring: Late spring, summer and early fall are preferable. There is little traffic. Follow the route to avoid prevailing winds.

This tour of rural Marin County gives the cyclist rugged ridges, redwood forested canyons, rolling grass and dairy lands. Via U.S. 101 and Sir Francis Drake Blvd., drive to the small community of Nicasio, the best place to start your trip. There is ample parking next to the baseball field across the street from Nicasio Ranch. Nicasio is a favorite taking-off spot for bicycle clubs so expect to see other cyclists. You should plan to carry your lunch as there are no restaurants en route and few stores where you can buy food.

To avoid prevailing winds, follow the route clockwise, The first major hill to be encountered is about three miles out of Nicasio. It is hard, so take your time. And when you reach the top there is a rewarding downhill run that whirls you right down to the San Geronimo National Golf Course.

A short distance from here you join Sir Francis Drake Blvd. This is the stretch where you will encounter the most traffic. The road follows the canyons of San Geronimo and Lagunitas Creeks.

You pass through Forest Knolls, picturesque Lagunitas, and Samuel P. Taylor State Park. The park has a magnificent virgin redwood grove, near which the first paper mill on the Pacific Coast was built in 1856 by Taylor. The mill's foundations are preserved. Just in-

side the park there is a pipe sticking out from the road cut. The water it carries is from a spring and gives a thirsty, hot cyclist a cold, refreshing drink. There are restrooms at park headquarters and, if you have time for a dip, there is a swimming hole.

Here you have a chance to shorten your trip, cutting it to 20 miles instead of 30. Plan to eat lunch at Samuel P. Taylor and, instead of climbing Bolinas Ridge, turn right and follow Platform Bridge Road.

If you continue the longer version of the tour, the second major uphill climb pushes you up to the crest of Bolinas Ridge, where you have a fine panorama of the Point Reyes Peninsula and Tomales Bay. Go through Olema, cross State 1 and ride to the park headquarters of Point Reyes National Seashore. This is an excellent lunch stop, with tables located under shady trees near the upper parking lot. Restrooms are available and information about Point Reyes can be acquired at the headquarters.

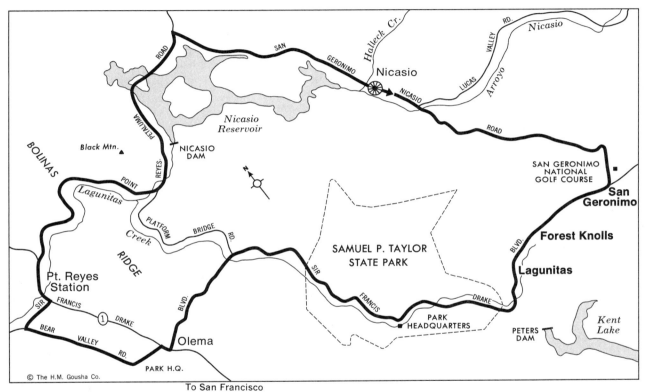

To San Francisco

Follow the route back to State 1 and Point Reyes Station. If you are traveling on a weekday or Saturday be sure to stop and browse through the old-fashioned general store.

The Point Reyes-Petaluma Road cuts through Bolinas Ridge, following the Lagunitas Creek Canyon. Although the road is mostly uphill until you pass Nicasio Dam, there usually is a strong tailwind helping you along. This tailwind will carry you around Nicasio Reservoir and back to your starting place.

A good, inexpensive after-ride snack and an invigorating swim await at the Nicasio Ranch. After your swim, you may even want to hang around for dinner at the ranch.

Point Reyes—Unchanged for Centuries

Approx. mileage: 40

Rating: A

Terrain: With the exception of one uphill grade over Inverness Ridge the terrain is flat and rolling.

Best times for touring: Good the year around but best when the countryside is spring-covered with new grass and wildflowers. You may encounter fog and strong winds on the ocean side of Inverness Ridge.

Point Reyes' environmental and ecological character has been unchanged for over 300 years. The peninsula is abundant with native plants, birds and wildlife that have ceased to exist in other areas of California now dotted with highrises and laced with freeways.

This tour of the Point Reyes National Seashore will give you a hint of what California was like before we began to settle here over 150 years ago. With the exception of an oyster farm, two overseas receiving stations, some dairy ranches and the two tiny communities of Bolinas and Inverness, natural growth goes on undisturbed.

Reach the park via State 1. Be sure to bring food with you as there is no place to eat inside Point Reyes National Seashore. An excellent place to begin your trip is the parking lot at the park headquarters. At the office pick up information about the sections of Point Reyes that are privately owned and the ones that are open to the public.

At the beginning of your ride you cycle along the marshlands and shores of Tomales Bay, a favorite for boating and sailing. There are good views of the Marin shoreline.

Inverness is the only community you will see on the whole tour. Nestled tightly against the tree-covered ridge, the quaint small town and its lush surroundings resemble the area for which it was named—Inverness, Scotland. The town was settled in the 1880's and the residents have successfully retained its quiet atmosphere.

Past the town you climb over Inverness Ridge and have mild continually rolling terrain for the rest of the trip. The wide views are magnificent—windswept pastures dotted with grazing cattle and a few white farm houses. The views are also minute—look closely and appreciate the beauty of the plant life, the rocks and the weathered fence posts softened with moss.

Continue along Sir Francis Drake Blvd. for glimpses of Drake's Estero and the curving shoreline of Drake's Bay. Here you see the site where in 1579 Drake careened and repaired his Golden Hinde for a return voyage to England after he had plundered the Spanish settlements of the New World. There were other historic landings also: Cermeno in 1595 and Limantour in 1841. From Drake's Beach there is a panoramic view of the coastline cliffs on the bay's opposite shore. Walk

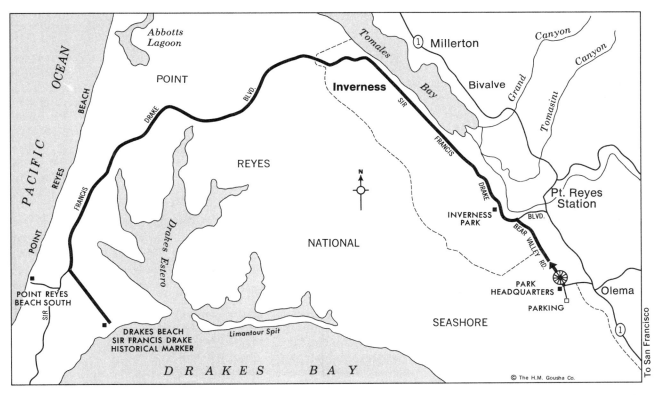

Abbotts Lagoon

POINT

Inverness

PACIFIC OCEAN

POINT REYES BEACH

Drakes Estero

REYES

NATIONAL

Tomales Bay

① Millerton

Bivalve

Grand Canyon

Tomasini Canyon

Canyon

Pt. Reyes Station

INVERNESS PARK

PARK HEADQUARTERS

PARKING

Olema

SEASHORE

POINT REYES BEACH SOUTH

DRAKES BEACH SIR FRANCIS DRAKE HISTORICAL MARKER

Limantour Spit

D R A K E S   B A Y

© The H.M. Gousha Co.

To San Francisco

①

BLVD.

DRAKE

SIR FRANCIS

DRAKE

BLVD.

BEAR VALLEY RD.

along the shore and you come to the entrance to Drake's Estero. Across the water from you is Limantour Spit.

Ride back to the main road and take the road to Point Reyes Beach South. From here there is a spectacular view of the 12-mile beach that dominates this whole coastline.

Both Drake's Beach and Point Reyes Beach South make excellent lunch stops with water and restrooms. You must return to park headquarters along the same road you came on. If you finish your tour in the late afternoon you may want to enjoy dinner at one of the quaint restaurants in Inverness or at Chez Madeline which is near Point Reyes Station.

The Occidental-Bodega Bay Loop

Approx. mileage: 38

Rating: B

Terrain: Flat and rolling.

Best times for touring: A pleasant trip all year round except on very cold days.

The Occidental-Bodega loop takes you to the coast for a seafood lunch and back to Occidental for a famous Italian dinner. It is a tour of the coastal rural areas and the resorts of the lower Russian River.

It is best to follow the route counterclockwise so you can bicycle along the ocean side of State 1 and take advantage of the prevailing winds. Occidental, highest community along the route, will serve as a starting point for this trip. Actually, it can begin from any of the towns along the way. But if you want to take advantage of Occidental's well-known family-style Italian restaurants, start there and return for dinner.

Take Bohemian Highway north and follow it and Main Street into Monte Rio. The road is fairly level, narrow and winding as it follows the course of Dutch Bill Creek down to Russian River. There is little traffic.

Moscow Road is a narrow lane along the southern bank of the river. Cross the river at Duncan Mills where you may want to rest and buy a snack at the small country store.

State 116 is fairly wide and has shoulders along some stretches, so bicycling is fairly easy. Although you are cycling downhill there may be headwinds to slow you down.

After turning onto State Highway 1 and crossing the bridge there is an uphill grade and then rolling terrain along the coast until you reach Bodega Bay. On windy days a tailwind will help speed you along the highway. It is heavily traveled and not too wide, so bicyclists should be careful of the traffic.

An excellent lunch stop is at Bodega Bay—the cafes near the harbor feature seafood. But, if you prefer picnicking, there are tables, water and restrooms at the Sonoma Coast State Beach Park Headquarters. After lunch walk along Salmon Creek Beach and enjoy the rolling surf. The road to Bodega takes you near the northern edges of Estero Americano. On reaching Bodega you'll find the old town has plenty of character in its quaint old buildings.

The road from Bodega back to Occidental follows the upstream course of Salmon Creek. The grass-covered hillsides slowly give way to trees as you cycle further inland. After passing through Freestone the road winds its way up the creek and takes you back to Occidental.

If you return to Occidental around dinner time you may want to have an excellent family style dinner at one of Occidental's famous restaurants. If you return after 5 p.m. you may have to wait for dinner but the happy tourist crowds, pleasant atmosphere and foods are worth it.

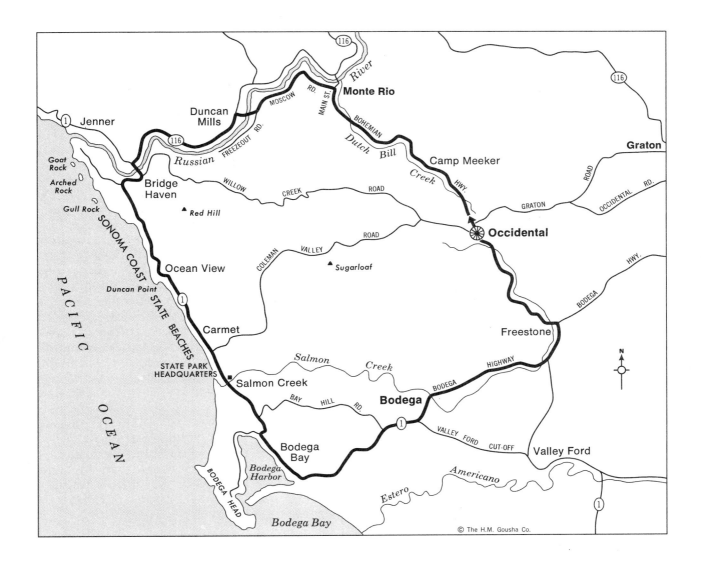

Russian River Ramble

Approx. mileage: 35

Rating: A

Terrain: Wooden hill country and flat grasslands. Some headwinds on return route down Main River Road.

Best times for touring: Any time of year is good except the extremely cold, rainy winter.

Old river resorts, redwoods, rural backroads and wineries are highlights of this tour through the Russian River country. With its rustic buildings, quaint tourist atmosphere and surrounding forested hillsides, Guerneville has become the center of the Russian River resort area. Make it your starting point by driving along the river on State 116 from State 1, or on River Road off U.S. 101.

As you leave Guerneville on Main Street you see the wide river below you. Continuing along, you pass through the old resort area where, in pre-World War II decades, half the families in San Francisco migrated annually to catch the sun. The numerous cabins are nestled among the redwood covered slopes. This is Rio Nido.

Around the bend is the Korbel Champagne Cellars. Don't stop for tasting now—save it for the trip back. This stretch of River Road is wide and heavily traveled, but there is a wide shoulder in most areas.

Be sure to turn onto Westside Road just before the bridge over the river. Do not cross the river. The turn is so unnoticeable that you might cycle past. Narrow, hilly and winding, the road is a little traveled lane that takes you into Healdsburg.

Panoramic views of the vast agricultural lands and the far mountain ranges are to the east. Along the route itself are redwoods, grasslands, orchards, vineyards and old farm houses. As you cycle north the roadway is on the western slopes of the valley. Santa Rosa and Healdsburg can be seen spread across the valley floor.

Healdsburg provides an excellent lunch stop. There are several cafes in the business district or you may picnic in the downtown park on green lawns under shady trees.

The Old Redwood Highway starts your route home. Just south of Healdsburg is the new Windsor Winery rising out of the vineyards. Stop for some wine tasting and conversation with the vintners. The winery is open every day from 11 a.m. to 5 p.m.

Turn off Old Redwood Highway at Eastside Road, that takes you through grassy and wooded pasturelands. Along the western hillsides you have glimpses of the climbing Westside Road you rode on to Healdsburg. From the high point at the junction of Eastside and Trenton-Healdsburg

Roads there is an excellent view westward down the Russian River as it pushes along toward the ocean. River Road carries you through thick trees again. The road is not very wide and there is plenty of traffic, so take care.

Expect to be slowed down somewhat after you cross the bridge and cruise down River Road. You may encounter some headwinds. But soon Korbel Cellars appears and you may stop for the treat you promised yourself. Korbel is open daily with tours at 1 and 2:30 p.m. between June 15 and September 15. From the winery it is just a short jog back to Guerneville.

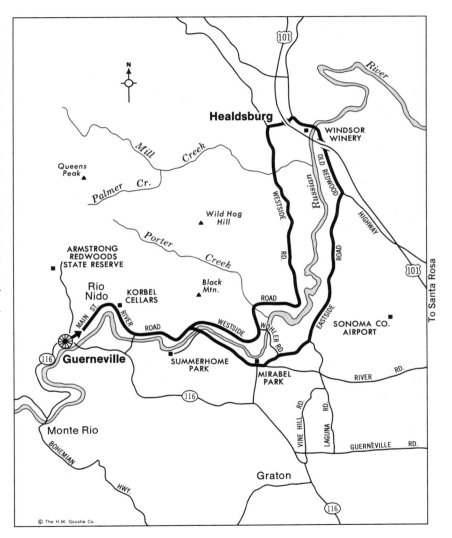

Healdsburg—Geyserville Loop

Approx. mileage: 30

Rating: B

Terrain: Mostly level.

Best times for touring: Any time of the year.

The Dry Creek and Alexander Valley areas are the highlights of this tour through the rural Sonoma County countryside. When beginning the trip in Healdsburg cycle out Dry Creek Road. It begins as a wide avenue as it passes under the freeway and through agricultural lands, becoming a narrow road as it continues into the back country. There is no traffic on Dry Creek and the only noises you hear are the birds, a cow or two, the clicking of sprockets and the tires on the road. The countryside is a mixture of fields, shrubs and trees. There is a pleasant feeling cycling along in silence.

The only tough section of this tour is on Canyon Road as you pass over the ridge separating the Dry Creek drainage from the Russian River. The climb is steep but there are panoramic views of the Russian River and Alexander Valley from the crest, and a rewarding downhill run to State 101.

This one-mile stretch along the highway into Geyserville is narrow and heavily traveled. There is no shoulder so bicyclists should be alert and careful of the traffic.

There is a small old-fashioned soda fountain on the right side of the highway as you enter Geyserville. If you want a picnic lunch bring it or buy it at the store and have a leisurely picnic down at the bridge while enjoying the scenery. This first bridge across the Russian River offers views of the wide river and the heavily wooded banks.

The roads through Alexander Valley are narrow, flat and have little traffic. State 128 and Red Winery Road take you through lush orchards and vineyards. In several areas trees shade the roadway.

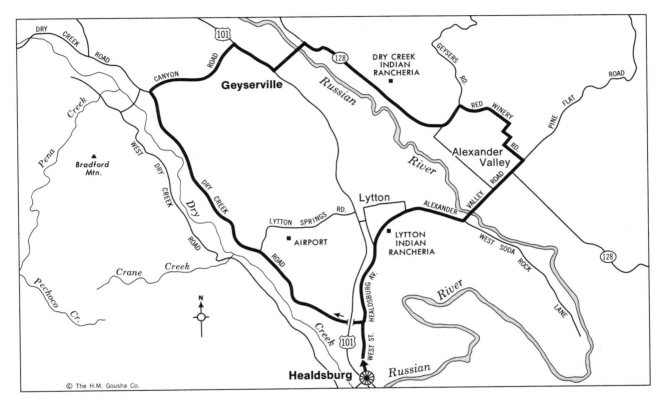

© The H.M. Gousha Co.

When Alexander Valley Road takes you across the Russian River again you may want to stop, wade and cool off. While there, you may see canoers passing by down-river to Healdsburg.

After cooling your feet in the river follow Alexander Valley Road and Healdsburg Avenue back into Healdsburg. This entire area is noted for its apples and grapes, and great quantities are shipped annually. Both Gey- serville, gateway to the geysers resort area that was popular years ago, and Healdsburg were settled in 1852 and became trading centers.

Wine, General Vallejo and Jack London

Approx. mileage: 43

Rating: A

Terrain: The southern part of this trip is relatively flat. In a few stretches there is the possibility of mild headwinds. The extreme northern branch runs over rolling hills with short climbs and descents.

Best times for touring: This is a good tour any time of year, especially when the hills are green in spring and the grapes are ripe in the fall.

A pastoral junket that encompasses a good chunk of California's Mexican histroy, this tour also takes in part of the wine country. The one and only starting place for the trip is Sonoma State College. (Take the Petaluma Blvd. exit north off U.S. 101.) It is best to travel counterclockwise so the hilly section will be at the end of the tour.

Leave the campus on Petaluma Hill Road. There is little traffic here and on Adobe Hill Road. You are surrounded by flat grass lands and the 2,295-foot crest of Sonoma Mountain bulges up to the left. Soon you approach a huge early California style building—the Petaluma Adobe, built by General Mariano Vallejo in the 1830's when the Mexican government named him head of this northernmost outpost of Mexican development. The holdings originally were 66,000 acres, but have been pared down to considerably less and established as the Petaluma Adobe State Historical Park. The lovely, cool verandas of the old home make an excellent stop. Open daily from 10 a.m. to 5 p.m., admission 25 cents for a self-guided tour.

Stage Gulch Road is narrow and heavily traveled, taking you into the southern tip of the Valley of the Moon. Ride left on E. Watmaugh, again turning left onto Arnold Drive.

Follow the route via Leveroni Road, Eighth Street East and Old Winery Road to the Buena Vista Winery. Nestled into the Sonoma hillside the Buena Vista is the oldest winery in California. Agoston Haraszthy, a Hungarian nobleman, imported European grape stock to the area and pioneered the wine industry. An influential business man he was also tied into the politics of the period. Two of his sons married two of General Vallejo's daughters.

Enter the old stone winery and follow the self-guided tour into the tunnels and the tasting room. Make sure that the lunch you bring along goes well with the excellent Buena Vista wine on sale here. There is a pleasant, shaded picnic area in front.

More history? More wine? After lunch, stop off at the Sebastiani Winery and then follow the route into historic Sonoma. The Plaza is ringed with interesting sights—the Bear Flag Monument (Sonoma was the scene of the 1846 uprising); Sonoma Barracks, built in 1836 by the General; Mission San Francisco Solano, last of the chain of 21 Franciscan missions. There is a fine exhibit of watercolors of all the missions by early artist Christopher Jorgensen. The Plaza also has gift and antique shops for browsing.

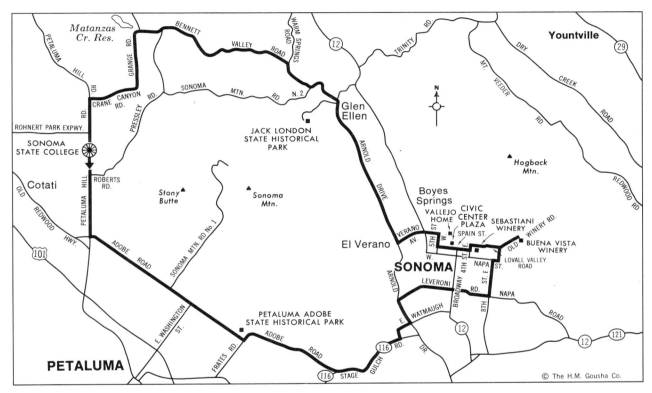

© The H.M. Gousha Co.

As you continue the tour on narrow Arnold Drive, be especially aware of the traffic. It is heavy and moves fast. Sonoma State Hospital has pleasant green lawns and just before you enter Glen Ellen There are several interesting ancient build- ings in this area. If you take the steep uphill climb to Jack London State Park you will see the remains of Wolf House, some of London's mementos and his collection of South Pacific art. Open daily from 10 a.m. to 5 p.m. 25 cents.

The last leg of the tour carries you along narrow roads through rolling hills and small picturesque valleys. Crane Canyon Road gives a good long downhill coast back to the flatlands at Sonoma State College.

Silverado Trail—Vive le Vin!

Approx. mileage: 22 (42 miles with Calistoga loop)

Rating: C (B with additional 20 miles)

Terrain: Flat with a few gentle grades through the heart of the wine country.

Best times for touring: This is an excellent all-year tour.

Through the vineyards to numerous wineries, enjoying husky samples as you go—this could be one of bicycling's premium tours. The Napa Valley is the richest and the most famous wine producing region of California. This trip takes you from Yountville to St. Helena, with an optional Calistoga loop.

Vintage 1870 in Yountville is an excellent starting place. An old, converted winery, Vintage 1870 now houses a group of shops selling handcrafts, gifts and antiques. Yountville is nestled at the southern end of the grape growing country and may be reached by Interstate 80 and State 29.

Yountville Cross Road is a quiet lane that takes you across the valley to the historic Silverado Trail. Edging the eastern side of the valley, the Silverado Trail received its name from the silver and quicksilver mines in the nearby mountains.

The traffic on Silverado Trail is light but fast moving and the roadway has shoulders to make cycling easier.

Pratt Avenue takes you into the heart of Napa's wine country: St. Helena. Ride across the old arched stone bridge, one of more than 60 that are characteristic of the wine country.

Just north of St. Helena there are three famous wineries that offer tours and tasting: Beringer, Christian Brothers and Charles Krug. Up the road from the wineries is the Freemark Abbey and the Hurd Candle Factory. Hundreds of candles are on display for sale at the factory, and on weekdays you can see how they are made.

Next door is a gourmet shop to load you with cheese and other delectables to go with your wine at lunch. Another excellent source for cheese and salami is the old white Olive Oil Factory on McCorkle Avenue in south-eastern St. Helena. For your picnic settle down on the shaded lawn of Lyman Park next to the city hall.

The 20-mile Calistoga loop is for those who want a longer trip before lunch. Do not turn on Pratt Avenue but continue on the Silverado Trail to Calistoga.

Returning to St. Helena on State 29 you pass the old Bale Mill, a prominent historical site with its towering water wheel and gigantic grinding wheels.

The last two wineries to visit are Louis Martini and the Heitz Cellars on the south end of town. Martini offers both a tour and tasting; at Heitz there is tasting only. (Most wine tours are similar and you need not take in every one you see. But stop at all tasting rooms.)

After leaving Heitz you should be feeling quite relaxed and loose. Zinfandel Lane (an appropriate name) takes you back to the Silverado Trail, a better route than the heavily traveled highway if your day's adventures have left you a little wobbly.

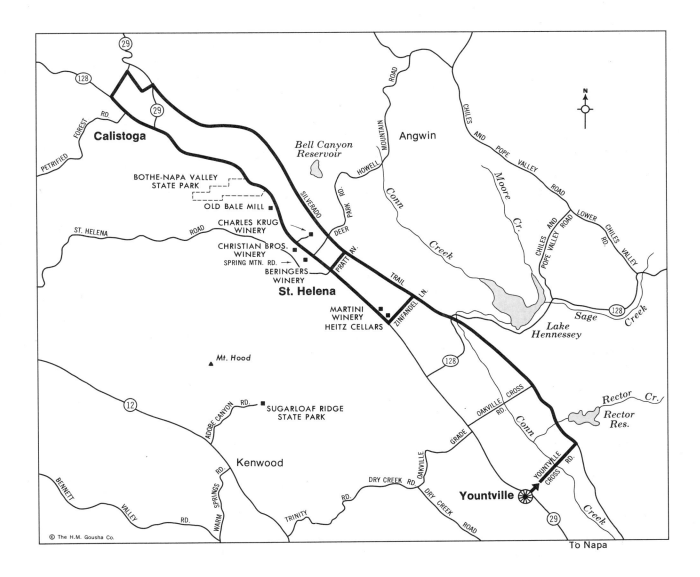

29

128

29 RD.

FOREST RD.

PETRIFIED

Calistoga

128

ST. HELENA

ROAD

BOTHE-NAPA VALLEY
STATE PARK

OLD BALE MILL ■

CHARLES KRUG
WINERY

CHRISTIAN BROS.
WINERY

SPRING MTN. RD. →

BERINGERS
WINERY

St. Helena

MARTINI
WINERY
HEITZ CELLARS

SILVERADO

DEER PARK RD.

PRATT AV.

TRAIL

ZINFANDEL LN.

*Bell Canyon
Reservoir*

HOWELL MOUNTAIN ROAD

Angwin

Conn

Creek

CHILES AND POPE VALLEY ROAD

Moore Cr.

CHILES AND POPE VALLEY ROAD

LOWER CHILES VALLEY RD.

128

Sage Creek

*Lake
Hennessey*

▲ *Mt. Hood*

12

ADOBE CANYON RD.

■ SUGARLOAF RIDGE
STATE PARK

Kenwood

BENNETT

VALLEY RD.

WARM SPRINGS RD.

TRINITY

RD.

DRY CREEK RD

OAKVILLE

DRY CREEK ROAD

128

OAKVILLE CROSS RD.

GRADE

Conn

YOUNTVILLE CROSS RD.

Yountville

29

Rector Cr.

*Rector
Res.*

Creek

To Napa

© The H.M. Gousha Co.

N

Two Tours from Pope Valley

Approx. mileage: 44—to Middletown and back, 36—Lake Berryessa loop.

Rating: A

Terrain: Flat and rolling, with a major grade on the Middletown tour and two on the Berryessa ride.

Best times for touring: Good all year. Best in late fall, winter and early spring when tourists are out of season at Berryessa.

Pope Valley is the common starting place for two rural tours that can be undertaken separately or combined to make one long trip. You can decide at the end of the first loop if you want to tackle the other.

The Berryessa loop is first. Park at the right of Eakle's store and take Chiles and Pope Valley Road through rolling pastoral lands. There are open green fields with grazing cattle and stretches of road shaded by trees covered with gray-green Spanish moss.

A three-mile sprint on State 128 takes you through more pastures and the woodlands of lower Chiles Valley. There is a long downhill grade following Soda and Capell Creeks to Lake Berryessa. The grade is especially steep after you turn off State 128 onto the Berryessa Knoxville Road.

The narrow, heavily traveled road stays a distance from the lake for the most part. The countryside is covered with shrubs and scattered pines (and dry grass, if you are a summer-fall rider).

Lakeshore picnic tables for a lunch stop will be found just north of the park headquarters. After lunch, there is swimming, sunbathing or just relaxing on the green lawns. If you swim, you will have to wear your suit on the trip because there are no easily accessible restrooms for changing clothes.

There is another climb as Pope Canyon Road follows the creek back to town. You notice the change in landscape from the dry lake region to the lush green of Pope Valley.

The Middletown tour also begins at Eakle's store and gets out of town on Pope Valley Road north. The backroads used for touring rural Napa and Lake Counties are narrow and traffic is nearly non-existent.

After the Aetna Springs turn-off there is a long, winding up-hill climb. Get in low gear and take your time. And if you tire—walk. The climb takes you into Butts Canyon. Until you pass Detert Reservoir the terrain has its ups and downs. Beyond the reservoir the landscape becomes a grassy plateau spotted with shrubs and pines, and blanketed with fresh, clean air.

The Middletown High School lawn is a good lunch place. Either bring your lunch or buy food at the store down the street. Restrooms at local gas stations. The return to Pope Valley is along the roads you just traveled.

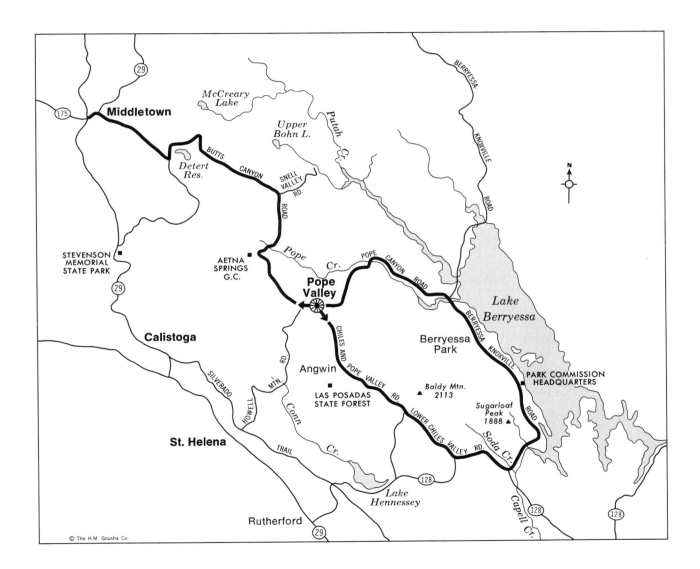

Pinole Valley-Martinez Loop

Approx. mileage: 30

Rating: B

Terrain: Rolling countryside with twisting roads on the northeastern leg of the trip.

Best times for touring: A good tour all year, it is at its best in the spring when the hillsides are green.

The starting point for this tour can be anywhere along the route. However, during weekends the Pinole Valley High School just south of U.S. 80 serves as a good takeoff spot.

The suburban stretch of Pinole Valley Road is wide and well-traveled at times. Cycling east, you find the road narrowing as it traces the course of Pinole Creek into the rural areas of Contra Costa County. Good views of the tree-fringed slopes of the surrounding hillsides are the feature of this leg of the junket.

Alhambra Valley Road offers you an old-time schoolhouse, a Christmas tree farm and an old-fashioned barnyard for pigs.

A hilly section appears east of the intersection with Bear Creek Road. There are a couple of sizeable grades, but the last twisting downhill run is a pleasure as you leave the winding canyon and shoot out into open orchard country. The road makes a left turn that leads you into Martinez.

Martinez, a good lunch stop, offers some interesting sightseeing. As you pass under the freeway (State 4) you see to the west the John Muir National Historical Site. John Muir, ardent conservationist, was founder of the Sierra Club. The house was built in 1882 and still is furnished in the styles of the last century. There are tours every hour from 10 a.m. to 4 p.m. daily except Monday. Admission is 50 cents; children under 16, free. Next to the Muir home is the Vicente Martinez adobe which was built in 1849.

A dandy picnic spot is on the corner of Talbert and Buckey. The Martinez Municipal Park (Rankin Park) has an excellent picnic area with lawns, shade trees, tables and restrooms.

Pomona Street is winding and narrow and takes you along the southern shores of the Carquinez Straits. High above the shoreline the road presents a sweeping view of the rolling, grassy hillsides, Suisun Bay and the delta country to the east.

Port Costa is just a short loop trip from Pomona Street. The old bayside town has a small harbor and quaint shops for browsing. From there you ride into Crockett, site of a huge C & H Sugar refinery and the south end of the Carquinez Bridges.

Multi-laned San Pablo Avenue takes you from Crockett back to Pinole. Between the two towns there are several uphill climbs. From the high vantage points there are good views of San Pablo Bay. Hurry by the pastel-painted Union 76 refinery. The smell is overpowering. When you reach the old downtown section of Pinole follow Pinole Valley Road back to the starting place at the high school.

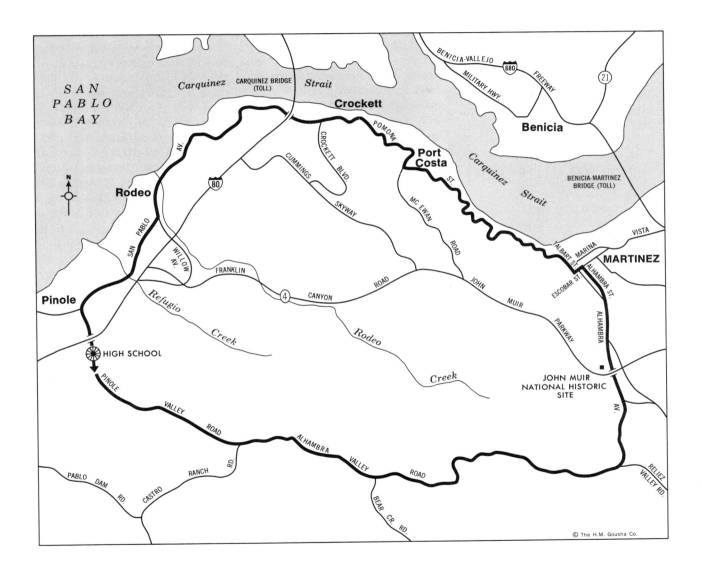

Trip To Fruit Picking Country

Approx. mileage: 36

Rating: B

Terrain: The countryside is mostly flat, except on the western leg of the trip where there are rolling hills with grades. You will also occasionally be buffeted with mild headwinds.

Best times for touring: Good all year, but best in early spring when the hills are lush green, in June during cherry picking season, and August when the peaches are ripe. There is very little traffic on most of the trip.

This tour will give you a good day of bicycling and will take you through the agricultural and pastoral lands of rural eastern Contra Costa County. With Brentwood as a starting point you can make the tour as long or short as you wish.

A good departure point in Brentwood is the city park. If you have not brought lunch, pick up some snacks at a local grocery store. There are no cafes or stores along the route.

As you leave Brentwood, turning east on Balfour Road and then left on Byron Highway, you pass by orchards and open fields, presenting a view of the vast agricultural lands that dominate this area. Look westward and you see Mount Diablo standing a majestic 3,849 feet high in the distance.

Leaving Delta Road, the tour takes you on State Route 4 for a half mile. Here is the heaviest traffic on the trip, but there is a narrow shoulder you can follow. Then, Lone Tree Way leads you through softly rolling grasslands, past the Antioch Airport.

Time for a lunch stop. Conveniently, Contra Loma Regional Park appears right on cue with sweeping lawns, picnic tables, restrooms and water. If you look skyward towards the east you may see skydivers in the distance gliding earthward. During warm weather bring your swimsuit and plunge into the Contra Loma Reservoir. A good swim will give you the pep to finish the trip.

A long, gradual climb is ahead. Shift to low gear on Empire Mine Road and enjoy yourself as you wander uphill through pastoral scenery. Deer Valley Road offers some up and down rolling terrain which is tiring uphill but a riding pleasure as you whizz downhill.

Marsh Creek Road carries you along the canyon floor as it widens to meet the broad flat agricultural plain. You will pass the home of the early California pioneer and physician, Dr. John Marsh. Poor John met a violent end from multiple stabbing in 1856.

Orchards line Walnut Blvd. all the way back to Brentwood. If, after you load your bike, thoughts of those tree-ripened cherries or peaches keep returning, drive back to the orchards for a supply to take home. If the day is hot, you might even like another swim at the regional park before going home.

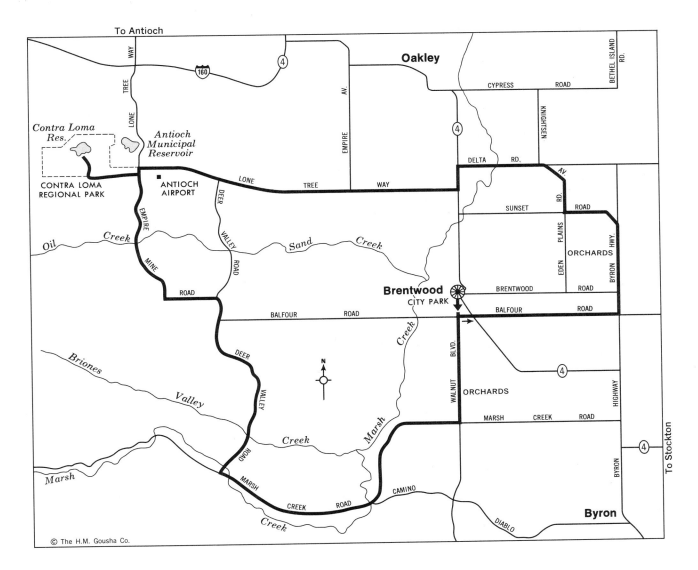

To Antioch

Oakley

160

4

BETHEL ISLAND RD.

WAY

TREE

LONE

CYPRESS ROAD

EMPIRE AV.

KNIGHTSEN

Contra Loma Res.

Antioch Municipal Reservoir

4

DELTA RD.

CONTRA LOMA REGIONAL PARK

ANTIOCH AIRPORT

LONE TREE WAY

AV.

RD.

SUNSET ROAD

Oil Creek

EMPIRE

DEER

Sand Creek

EDEN PLAINS

ORCHARDS

BYRON HWY.

MINE

VALLEY

ROAD

ROAD

Brentwood

BRENTWOOD ROAD

CITY PARK

Briones

BALFOUR ROAD

Creek

BALFOUR ROAD

Valley

DEER

N

WALNUT BLVD.

4

Creek

VALLEY

ORCHARDS

HIGHWAY

Marsh

ROAD

Marsh

MARSH CREEK ROAD

Creek

MARSH CREEK ROAD

CAMINO

4

To Stockton

BYRON

Creek

DIABLO

Byron

© The H.M. Gousha Co.

Cheese and Wine Picnic Tour

Approx. mileage: 35

Rating: B

Terrain: Flat and mildly rolling hills.

Best times for touring: Good all year except during the coldest months.

Rolling rural countryside, a world of clean fresh air, wild flowers, shady lanes, plus stops at a cheese factory and winery—these are features that make this tour a bicycling pleasure.

The taking off spot is Danville with Pleasanton and its cheese and wine spots as a lunchtime destination. (Actually, you could start from Pleasanton.) Drive Interstate 580 and 680 to Danville. As you cycle into the countryside on Camino Tassajara you pass through sweeping grassland and pastures with sheep and cattle grazing lazily. In the spring the entire countryside is covered with wildflowers dotting the green hills.

Tired? Rest a bit in the shade of the orchard trees at the corner of Tassajara and Highland Road. After Highland there is a gentle downhill run passing Camp Parks Regional Park and Santa Rita Rehabilitation Center (which was in the news during the U.C. Berkeley difficulties several years ago).

Whip down over the freeway (Int. 580) on Santa Rita Road into Pleasanton. You must contend with considerable traffic along here.

Make a few stops before lunch. The Pleasanton Cheese Factory offers over forty kinds of cheese for sampling and sale. Most of the varieties are pro-

duced at the factory on Main Street. After a good sampling and a purchase or two, you should make your next stop the Villa Armando Winery on St. John Street. With the cheese, a bottle of wine and some French bread in hand, proceed to the green lawns of the Railroad Park for an ideal on-the-road picnic lunch.

Leave Pleasanton on Hopyard Road, passing the Alameda County Fairgrounds. Traffic can be tight along here. When you cross over the freeway the road is called Dougherty. As you head north along this country road the slopes of Mount Diablo dominate the scenery in front of you and few cars will be seen. After crossing Tassajara, Blackhawk Road takes you past the southern entrance to Mount Diablo State Park. Ride along Diablo Road back to Danville.

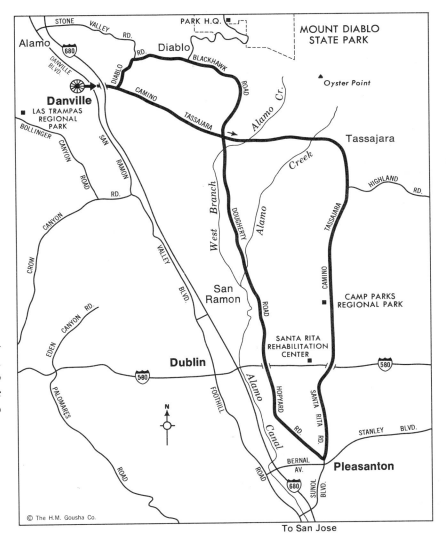

© The H.M. Gousha Co.

Palomares-Crow Canyon Loop

Approx. mileage: 42

Rating: A

Terrain: The western half of this tour is over rolling hill country while the eastern leg is relatively flat.

Best times for touring: Try to ride this tour in the spring when the wildflowers are blooming. Summers are quite hot.

The best location for starting your tour is the San Ramon Village Shopping Center at the corner of Amador and San Ramon Valley Roads in Dublin. Head north out of town along the San Ramon Valley Road. Bicycling is easy on this wide road. To the east is the broad valley with its intermingling grasslands and housing developments. To the west are rolling hills with clumps of trees dotting the landscape. In front of you the slopes of Mt. Diablo reach skyward.

As you ride along Crow Canyon Road you pass through orchards on both sides. For a short distance the road is wide but it narrows as you enter into rolling grasslands. You will meet very few cars along here.

The road becomes winding and in places tree-lined as you travel through this ranching area of Alameda County. As the road begins to follow Crow Creek you enter a canyon with tree-covered slopes. Around Crow Canyon Park there are several old-fashioned white fenced corrals along the route.

Lush green canyon walls dominate the route past the park. The road winds itself down until you enter East Castro Valley. Ride along two-lane East Castro Valley Blvd. and cross under the freeway (Int. 580) to Palo Verde Road.

A traditional one-room red schoolhouse is a landmark at the corner of Palo Verde and Palomares Road. This is the Palomares Public School built in 1868.

Palomares Road carries you into a beautiful little canyon where there is virtually no traffic. The west slopes are wooded and grassy. Small farmhouses edge up to the narrow roadside occasionally and cattle graze in small pastures. At the upper end of the valley is a long uphill climb. Walk it if you get tired. And take time to look back at the views.

From the crest a long steep downhill run twists through Stonybrook Canyon. The fern-edged creek and thick trees make a good resting spot for a tired cyclist.

Niles Canyon Road is narrow, flat and heavily traveled. In Sunol you can buy lunch and try out one of two good lunch stops. The first is the Sunol Water Temple situated in orchards just east of town. The second is at Bonita Park north of Sunol on Foothill Road. Both have picnic tables and shade trees but no restrooms.

Past Bonita Park the road is flat and as you approach Pleasanton the terrain opens up to the east forming the Livermore Valley. You pass through the western edge of Pleasanton where there is a mixture of rural and suburban areas with alternating woods, orchards, pastures and housing tracts. After crossing the freeway (Int. 580) you are back at the San Ramon Village Shopping Center.

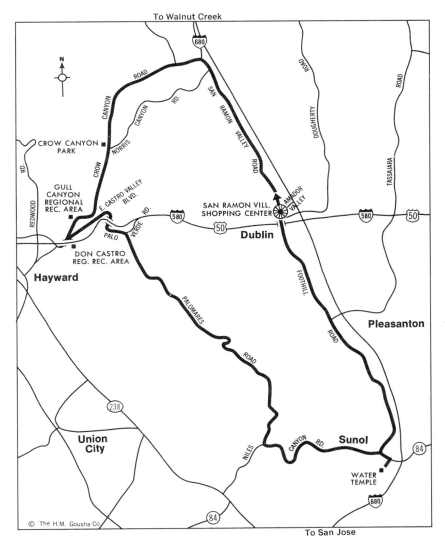

A Trio of Tours on the Delta

Approx. mileage: 25—Brannan Island, 22—Courtland-Clarksburg loop, 43—Rio Vista long loop.

Rating: C—Brannan Island, C—Courtland-Clarksburg, A—Rio Vista loop.

Terrain: Absolutely flat.

Best times for touring: Spring or fall. The summer heat is intense. Winds can be unpredictable and very strong.

Brannan Island tour starts in downtown Isleton, a small town on the Sacramento River. Terminous Road takes you south through rich agricultural country. The short stretch of State 12 is heavily traveled but wide.

Brannan Island Road travels under a bridge and along the traffic-free levee tops to State 160. Stop at the Pirate's Lair for a rest and a view of the active waterways.

A short stretch on State 160 takes you to Brannan Island State Recreational Area, a good lunch stop with shade trees and picnic tables. There are no stores, so you must carry your own food. Bring your swimming suit and relax for the afternoon swimming and sunbathing before you retrace your route. Take a shortcut at Jackson Slough Road to Terminous Road.

Courtland-Clarksburg loop starts at either town. If you take off from Courtland you cross the old picturesque drawbridge to Sutter Island. Another old bridge takes you to Merritt Island. Tom's Fountain at Jefferson and Courtland is a good place for a cool drink and a view of the delta landscape.

Continue on Jefferson to Clarksburg Road. If you happen to look westward and see the stack of a cargo ship, it's not a mirage. The vessel is following the Sacramento River deep-water ship channel to the Port of Sacramento. There are patches of shade trees along here, too— a blessing on a hot day.

Clarksburg has a restaurant if you have not brought your lunch. The green, shady lawn of the high school is a good picnic and rest spot.

The return to Courtland is along a levee road high above the Sacramento, which is busy with houseboats and other pleasure craft.

The Rio Vista longer delta tour starts at the riverside end of Main Street and circles Ryer Island, Courtland and Walnut Grove.

As you bicycle out of Rio Vista along the river you pass the giant dredges that work the river parked along the bank. Their huge rusting scoops are resting on the ground next to the road.

"The Real McCoy" ferry carries you across Cache Slough to Ryer Island. From the ferry there are excellent views down the river of the Rio Vista bridge, up Cache Slough and the tip of Grand Island.

The levee road on Ryer Island follows Cache and Miner Sloughs. The views are great. To the east is a patchwork of lush alfalfa fields and freshly cultivated earth.

As you bicycle northward you may encounter headwinds that will slow your pace.

But, what was once a headwind while cycling north becomes a tailwind as you head south along the Sacramento River levee near Courtland. Cross the picturesque drawbridge and head into Courtland for a lunch stop. Eat along the banks of the river and enjoy the views of the river and surrounding delta. Locke was established around 1915 by Chinese laborers and its population today is still entirely Chinese.

In Walnut Grove cross the graceful old drawbridge to Grand Island and on to the Howard Landing ferry, which takes you across Steamboat Slough and back to Ryer Island.

After recrossing the Ryer Island Ferry, return to Rio Vista. As you bicycle along there are scenic views of the river, the bridge and Brannan Island. All delta tours can be reached by driving U.S. 80 and State 12.

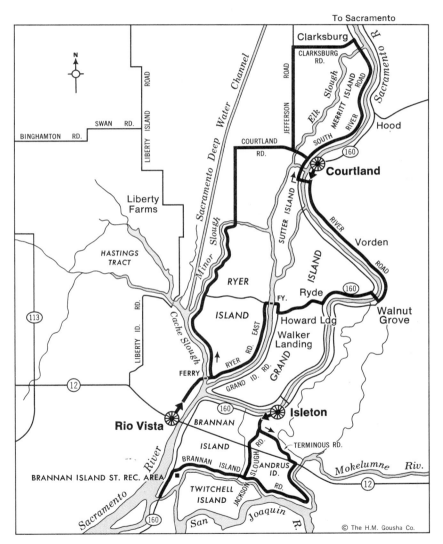

© The H.M. Gousha Co.

The Artichokes and Redwoods Circle

Approx. mileage: 28

Rating: B

Terrain: Flat to rolling hills with a few steep climbs on the eastern leg of the trip.

Best times for touring: Best when it isn't cold and windy, but a good tour anytime of year.

The artichoke fields of southern San Mateo County and the redwood covered slopes toward the east are traveled in this loop trip from San Gregorio State Beach.

Actually, you can begin the tour from any of the three towns on the route—Pescadero, La Honda or San Gregorio. Drive to the coastside towns via State 1 and get to La Honda from Skyline Blvd. (State 35) on State 84.

San Gregorio Beach has ample parking and a good view of the sweeping coastline. The distance to La Honda Road (State 84) is short but the Coast Highway is usually heavy with traffic. Cyclists should use extreme caution and may even want to walk the short distance.

La Honda Road is a wide road leading you into San Gregorio, a tiny community with attractive old buildings. If you have not brought your lunch drop in at one of the small groceries. There are no other stores until La Honda.

East of San Gregorio the road travels along the northern edge of the valley. The lower part is dominated with artichoke fields, memorable in late summer when the purple thistles are blooming. As you ride eastward the valley narrows gradually into a canyon with redwood forested slopes.

Nestled under the redwoods is La Honda (Spanish for "The Deep"). You'll enjoy riding through this lively community where there is a grocery store and several spots with refreshments. This is a resort community with many weekend homes deep in the redwoods—and with more permanent residents each year.

The redwood forest you wind through between La Honda and Loma Mar is characteristic of the woods that dominated the Northern California coastlands in the last century. The ground cover is a mixture of ferns, horsetails and numerous wildflowers adding their color in the spring. As you near the crest, Pescadero Road follows a ridge from which there are panoramic views. To the south can be seen the green tree tops of Butano Forest.

The downhill run is steep, winding and often shaded by redwoods. Near the bottom is an excellent lunch stop with picnic and restroom facilities; and hiking trails at San Mateo County Memorial Park.

Loma Mar is a little community with several overgrown dilapidated buildings. Out of town you follow the course of Pescadero Creek along the bot-

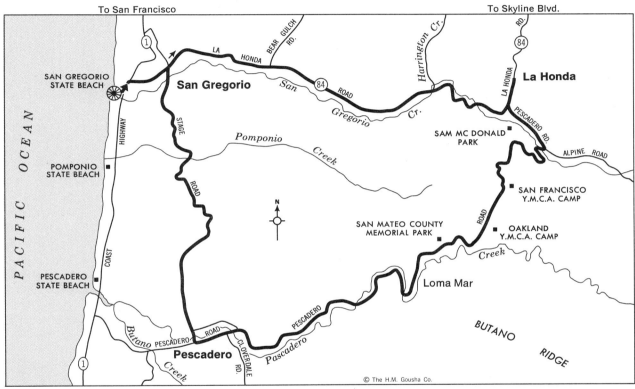

© The H.M. Gousha Co.

tom of a narrow valley. Stay on the main road and do not turn off on roads leading to the left.

Pescadero is a quiet town huddled in an expanse of artichoke fields. There is a quaint old church and an old cemetery just north of town on Stage Road that you might want to explore for a time.

Stage Road is a narrow old lane that takes you up over the twisting ridge to another valley. There are some mild grades and several hairpin turns on the downhill. Be careful. Ride through San Gregorio and back to the beach.

Stanford-Water Temple Sprint

Approx. mileage: 30

Rating: B

Terrain: Flat to rolling hills. Heavy traffic on Canada Road stretch of Interstate 280. Campus and residential streets are fairly flat.

Best times for touring: A fine tour anytime but best when the wind isn't blowing.

Stanford University is the starting place for a loop through quiet Woodside, the Pulgas Water Temple and back past San Mateo County suburbs. Actually, you may begin your ride any place along the route but Stanford University Quad is a well known landmark.

Cycle through campus along Serra to Lomita; left on Campus and right on Lasuen until you reach Mayfield Avenue. This connects with Junipero Serra Blvd., taking you past Lake Lagunita and Stanford Golf Course. Turn left at Alpine Road where there is a traffic light. Along the east side of the roadway is a bicycle path that goes under Interstate 280 Freeway and almost all the way into Portola Valley.

Portola Road starts a long downhill run through the beautiful valley. Along the route are lovely homes, picturesque roadside businesses and clusters of redwood trees. To the west the forested slopes stretch skyward.

After passing Searsville Lake turn right onto Mountain Home Road and ride along the shady lane past country homes and horseback riders into Woodside. You can buy lunch items at Roberts of Woodside on the corner of Mountain Home and Old County Road. Or, take a few minutes out for a cup of coffee at the cafe across the street where the parking lot is often as filled with horses as it is with cars.

Take off on Canada Road, a two-lane, lightly traveled road that passes downhill from Canada College. The road eventually blends into Interstate 280 (Junipero Serra—"The World's Most Beautiful Freeway") where it is still two-laned and traffic bound. The actual freeway strip is under construction.

There is a shoulder that gives ample room for a cyclist. This is pretty country—grassy fields, occasional deer and stands of towering, pungent eucalyptus.

When you reach Pulgas Water Temple be careful when crossing the highway. The classic style temple is surrounded with greenery and a reflecting pool. An excellent spot for a picnic lunch.

Back down the same route to Edgewood Road, you will encounter a short, steep climb and be rewarded with a long downhill run on the eastern slope that leads into Redwood City. The Alameda de las Pulgas carries you through suburban Redwood City, Atherton (more horses and fields) and the western part of Menlo Park.

The big Stanford Shopping Center is on the route just off Willow Road. Turn right on Arboretum. And right again to ride in a canyon of palm trees down Palm Drive to the Stanford Quad.

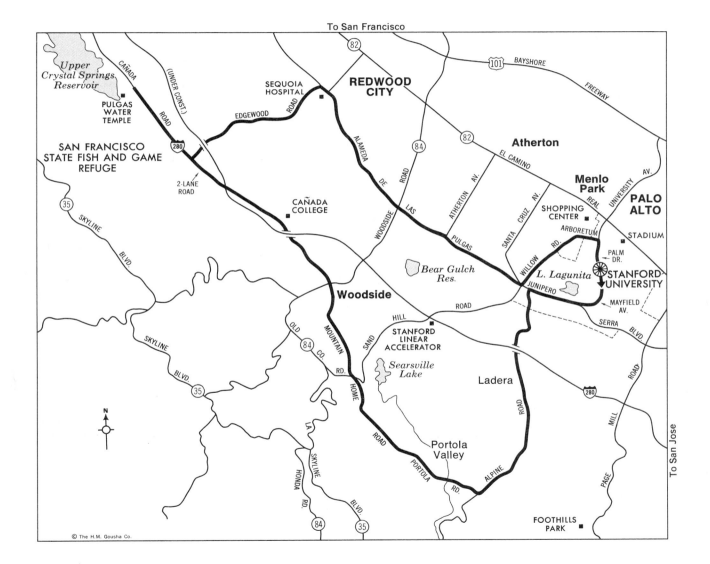

To San Francisco

Upper Crystal Springs Reservoir

PULGAS WATER TEMPLE

SAN FRANCISCO STATE FISH AND GAME REFUGE

CAÑADA ROAD

(UNDER CONST.)

280

2-LANE ROAD

EDGEWOOD ROAD

SEQUOIA HOSPITAL

REDWOOD CITY

82

101 BAYSHORE FREEWAY

82

84

Atherton

EL CAMINO

Menlo Park

PALO ALTO

UNIVERSITY AV.

35

SKYLINE BLVD.

CAÑADA COLLEGE

ALAMEDA DE LAS PULGAS

WOODSIDE ROAD

ATHERTON AV.

SANTA CRUZ AV.

REAL

SHOPPING CENTER

ARBORETUM

STADIUM

PALM DR.

Bear Gulch Res.

WILLOW RD.

L. Lagunita

STANFORD UNIVERSITY

Woodside

JUNIPERO

ROAD

MAYFIELD AV.

SERRA BLVD.

OLD

84

MOUNTAIN CO. RD.

HOME

HILL

SAND

STANFORD LINEAR ACCELERATOR

Searsville Lake

Ladera

ROAD

ALPINE

280

MILL ROAD

SKYLINE BLVD.

35

LA HONDA RD.

SKYLINE BLVD.

ROAD

PORTOLA RD.

Portola Valley

PAGE

84

35

FOOTHILLS PARK

To San Jose

N

© The H.M. Gousha Co.

115

Alviso Adobe-Alum Rock Park Loop

Approx. mileage: 20

Rating: C

Terrain: Mostly flat, some hills on the Alum Rock excursion.

Best time for touring: Anytime.

You start this tour in San Jose and ride to the old Alviso adobe and Alum Rock Park. To get to the departure point, take the 13th Street exit from Bayshore Freeway (U.S. 101) and drive to the corner of Taylor Street. Get on your bike and back track down 13th, over Bayshore to Oakland Road.

Once known as Mission Road this was the route to the old San Jose Mission, important in San Jose history. After a short distance you bridge Coyote Creek. The Rancho Rincon de los Esteros was traversed lengthwise by this creek. The land was granted to Ygnacio Alviso in 1838 by Governor Alvardo.

From 1840 to 1843 Alviso was administrator of the Santa Clara Mission properties. He died in 1848.

After a few miles Oakland Road also becomes Main Street; turn right on Calaveras Blvd. and continue on along past the Milpitas City Hall and Civic Center to Piedmont Road. Near the intersection of these two streets is the Alviso Adobe. The battered dwelling marks an important site in the development of this area.

The surrounding lands comprised the Rancho Milpitas (maize fields). Two men, Jose Maria Alviso, son of Ygnacio Alviso, and Nicholas Berryessa, claimed the land.

Both men were active in the community and highly regarded. Berryessa held a high governmental office and Alviso in 1836 was the *alcalde* of the Pueblo de San Jose.

Berryessa suffered may hardships during the Bear Flag activities. Fremont plundered his cattle, his brother was killed and the land commission rejected his claim for Rancho Milpitas. He died insane in 1863.

In 1856 Alviso was granted the 4,457 acres of the Rancho Milpitas. The only remaining building of Alviso's original four adobes comprising his hacienda was probably built in the 1830's. The second story of this adobe is covered by modern weatherboarding to protect the original material. Alviso's house still stands in a colorful flower garden in the midst of fruit orchards. The ranch lands are still farmed.

After examining the adobe continue the tour down Piedmont Road. Ride on Piedmont for about three miles, then make a left on Penitencia. If you're tired, an alternate route can take you quickly back to the starting point and cut off about five miles. Go right on Penitencia, make a left on Capitol, then a quick right on Mabury Road to 13th Street.

If you've decided to finish the tour, follow Penitencia to Alum Rock Park. It's a good place to rest, eat lunch and do some exploring. Known as "Little Yosemite," for its natural rock formations, it also boasts 22 mineral springs.

To return to the departure point get on Alum Rock Avenue and follow it (the name changes to Santa Clara) to 13th Street.

At the corner of Santa Clara and 13th if you look to the left you'll see San Jose State College. Founded in 1851, it is the oldest non-private educational institution in California.

A right turn on 13th Street and a seven block ride will take you back to the beginning of your tour.

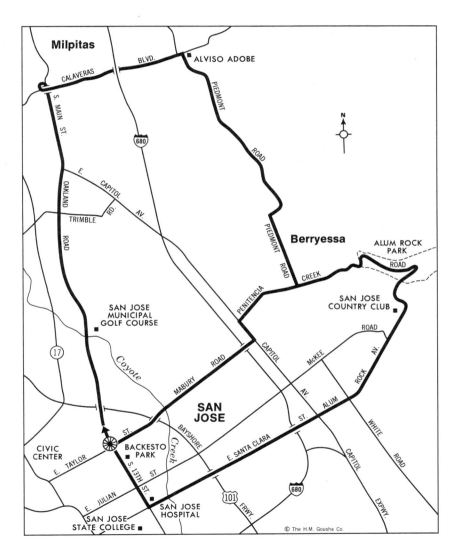

Ride the Mountain Charlie to Santa Cruz

Approx. mileage: 45

Rating: A

Terrain: Through the mountains there is a series of short, steep climbs connected with flat runs. You will encounter some traffic in the city of Santa Cruz.

Best times for touring: Good all year except in coldest part of winter.

Haul your bike up to Lexington Dam via State Highway 17. You can safely park near Santa Clara Boathouse or in the parking area provided by the park department about a quarter mile east of the dam. Be prepared with a snack, water and sweater—you're ready to strike out over the hills to Santa Cruz.

Contrary to your instincts, do not go west of Highway 17. Ride along the north shore of the reservoir on Alma Bridge Road to the mouth of Lime Kiln Canyon. A short detour up the canyon takes you to some of the old beehive-shaped kilns that gave the place its name.

Continue along the eastern edge of Lexington Reservoir on Alma Bridge Road. In about two and a half miles you pass through what appears to be a quarry at the mouth of Soda Springs Canyon. Actually, this is an active surface scar of the Soda Springs Fault, an offshoot and near relative of the San Andreas Fault.

At Aldercroft Heights Road cross the bridge and climb the hill to the so-called Old Los Gatos-Santa Cruz Road. Turn left up the highway. In about a half mile you enter Moody Gulch and cross a great slide. You are now in the San Andreas Fault. Shortly after, if you look over the bank you see a paralleling road grade and adjacent to it an older road—this is the *really* old Santa Cruz road.

At Patchen there is an historical monument. Turn right here on Mountain Charlie Road, known in the 1800's as the Santa Cruz Turnpike. This is probably the easiest route over the mountains but you require a gear of 40 inches (42-28) or lower. The Mountain Charlie is a typical old horse and wagon road with short, steep climbs connected with flat runs where the team could rest.

At the summit, cross over the "new" Santa Cruz Highway (State 17) on a viaduct. Cut to the left and ride southerly along the summit, dropping down past the ghost town of Glenwood (once a lumber center) toward Bean Creek Canyon.

Continue down Glenwood Drive and then right on the four-lane Old Santa Cruz Highway through Scotts Valley. Turn left at a traffic light and watch for Glen Canyon Road. Ride on into Santa Cruz on this road where it becomes Market Street and passes by De Laveaga Park, a good picnicking place.

Leave the city on Water Street and Soquel Avenue, crossing over State 1. You connect with Soquel-San Jose Road. Ride up the hill until you reach Summit Road, which takes you back to Patchen. Follow your original route around the reservoir.

To cut this tour into two easy pieces, plan on spending the night in Santa Cruz.

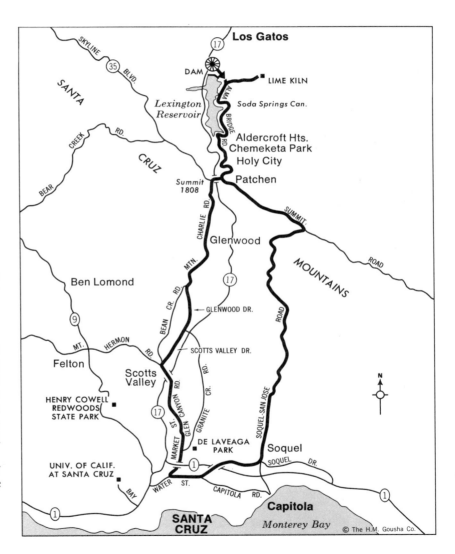

Other California Tours

(Selected by Paul Schwemler and Paul DeWitt)

Ride the One-Way Roads of Yosemite

Approx. mileage: 5—round trip from Yosemite Village to Mirror Lake. 12—round trip from the Village to Pohono Bridge.

Rating: C

Terrain: Mostly flat, with a few mild slopes.

Best times for touring: Good anytime the Valley floor is free of snow. Traffic can be a problem on North Valley Road and South Valley Road, especially on summer weekends. To explore the Valley at its uncrowded best, try visiting from mid-April through May (wildflowers and full waterfalls) or from mid-September through October (spectacular fall color). You may catch some nippy weather and heavy rains, but the lack of crowds makes it all worthwhile.

Bicycling in Yosemite Valley is much more enjoyable now than it was a few years ago. The entire east end of the Valley is closed to auto traffic, so cyclists can pedal along in peace except for an occasional shuttle bus.

And in the western part of the Valley, the roads are all one way, so that even when they are most crowded with cars and pickup campers, cyclists can pick their way along one shoulder or the other without much difficulty.

Bicycling is an excellent way to experience the beauty and grandeur of the Valley. The overall image of the high rock walls, waterfalls, meadows and wildlife is revealed much more vividly than it ever could be to motorists. This is particularly true for children, and fortunately, cycling is easy on the flat Valley floor.

The two tours shown on the map are short and if you do nothing but ride around the loops, they can be finished in short order. But that's not the way to enjoy Yosemite Valley. Instead, pack a picnic lunch and start out from Yosemite Village. Plan on spending a day on the road, stopping to throw a few rocks into the Merced River, enjoy the views, or take one of the short hikes to the waterfalls.

On the eastern loop, the natural stopping point is Mirror Lake. But you can also spend some time profitably at Happy Isles, one of the Valley's major trail heads and the location of a comprehensive information center. On the return leg, be sure to stop at Indian Cave, where you can clamber around on the rocks and imagine the days before the coming of white men. If you want to add some pleasant hiking to your cycling, leave the bikes at Mirror Lake and take the easy three-mile trail along Tenaya Creek. This isn't a very tiring walk, and it affords some spectacular new views of Half Dome.

The longer loop has a worthwhile stop in every half mile. There are many excellent guidebooks available for your use; perhaps the most practical is the official Yosemite Road Guide, which has keyed explanations to every important landmark, viewpoint, waterfall and historic site. With this in hand, just keep an eye out for the numbered markers along the road and you won't miss anything.

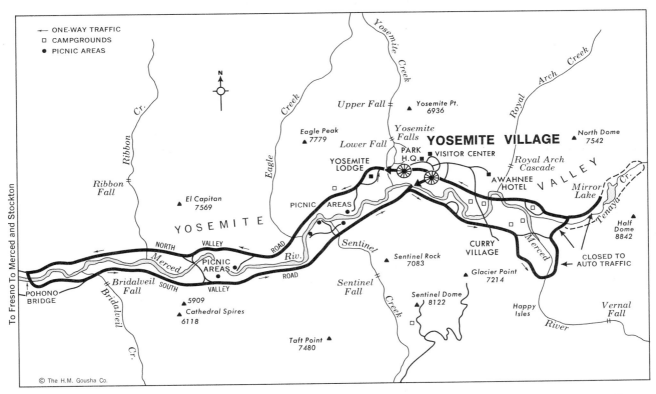

Map legend:
- ← ONE-WAY TRAFFIC
- □ CAMPGROUNDS
- ● PICNIC AREAS

N

Yosemite Creek

Royal Arch Creek

Ribbon Cr.

Eagle Creek

Upper Fall

Yosemite Pt. 6936

Eagle Peak ▲ 7779

Yosemite Falls

Lower Fall

PARK H.Q. ■

YOSEMITE VILLAGE

North Dome ▲ 7542

Royal Arch Cascade

VISITOR CENTER

Ribbon Fall

YOSEMITE LODGE

El Capitan ▲ 7569

AWAHNEE HOTEL

VALLEY

Mirror Lake

Tenaya Cr.

PICNIC AREAS

Half Dome 8842

Y O S E M I T E

CURRY VILLAGE

NORTH VALLEY

ROAD

Merced Riv.

Sentinel

Merced

CLOSED TO AUTO TRAFFIC

To Fresno To Merced and Stockton

PICNIC AREAS

ROAD

Sentinel Rock 7083

Glacier Point 7214

Bridalveil SOUTH VALLEY Fall

Sentinel Fall

Sentinel Dome 8122

Happy Isles

Vernal Fall

POHONO BRIDGE

Bridalveil Cr.

▲ 5909

▲ Cathedral Spires 6118

Sentinel Creek

River

Taft Point ▲ 7480

© The H.M. Gousha Co.

There are three excellent spots for lunch on this tour. At El Capitan, Yellow Pine and Rocky Point picnic areas, you can ride down to the edge of the Merced River and get away from most of the sights and sounds of vehicular traffic.

If you're making your first trip to Yosemite, spend some time at the main Visitor Center, where you can get a good introduction to the geology of the area, and learn something about the flora and fauna. Rangers on duty will tell you about the best view points and the trails best suited to your individual hiking abilities.

Accommodations range from the elegant Ahwahnee Hotel down to rustic cabins. Several campgrounds also are available. There is a full range of services at Yosemite Village and Curry Village, so you can easily replenish your food and clothing supplies.

123

Through the Redwoods by "Skunk" and Bike

Approx. mileage: 40 by rail and 36 more by bicycle.

Rating: A—from Willits to Fort Bragg. More difficult from Fort Bragg to Willits.

Terrain: Hilly, twisting downhill run from Willits to Fort Bragg.

Best times for touring: Preferably not during the summer tourist season. Best in spring or fall.

The famous Skunk train carries you and your bike halfway on this adventure through the spectacular redwoods and rolling hills of Mendocino County, from Fort Bragg to Willits.

During most of the year the best place to begin this journey is from the Fort Bragg depot of the California Western Railroad. At present there is little room to store bicycles on the Skunk rail cars, so the trip is limited to a maximum group of four cyclists. No bicycles are carried on the larger Super Skunk. The fare one way is $4.20. Reservations for bicycles and cyclists should be made at least a month in advance so the company can confirm the request. Total fare must accompany the request for reservations. Train schedules and prices are subject to change, so write to the California Western Railroad, Fort Bragg, Ca. 94537, for reservations and current prices and schedules.

Board the Skunk in Fort Bragg at 9:50 a.m. For the next one and three-quarter hours you will ride through majestic redwoods, orchards, fields of wildflowers and pastures with grazing cattle.

You arrive in time for lunch in Willits where there are several cafes. If you prefer picnicking, there is a small park with green lawns, tables and shady trees on Commercial Street just west of the Willits depot. After lunch you may want to have a short tour of the town.

As you bicycle out of Willits on State 20 you pass several lumber mills of the region. Lumbering is one of the major industries of California's northcoast counties. Past the lumber mills the road begins a long mild uphill grade.

After reaching the crest of the coast range there is a long 30-mile downhill run with four short uphill grades along the way. On some of the uphill grades you may want to get off and walk. The grades are steep in spots, so make sure your brakes are in good condition. During the week traffic is light but on weekends and in the summer season the tourists will be out crowding the narrow, twisting road. On the long downhill runs you may want to stop occasionally to give your hands a rest from working the brakes.

When the road contours around the hillsides there are numerous steep cuts along the way. Spectacular views can be seen from many high vantage points on the road. As you cycle toward the ocean and drop in elevation the trees become smaller and shorter, giving way

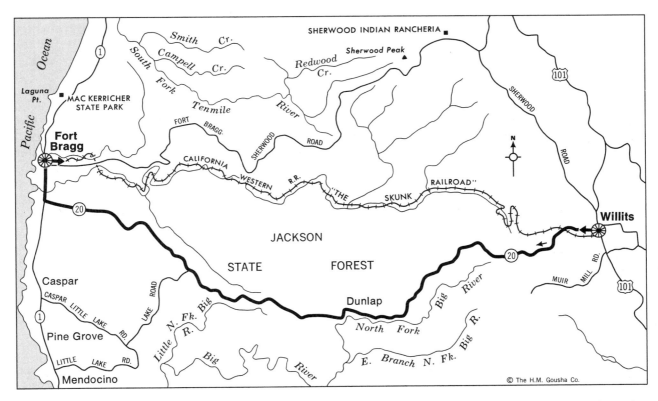

to shrubs and grasslands. You do not see the ocean until you are almost there. The road breaks out into rolling flat lands covered with grasses, shrubs and clumps of trees. The short distance along State Highway 1 into Fort Bragg is wide and easy to navigate.

During the summer (June 17 to September 9) you can begin this cycling adventure from Willits. Bicycle to Fort Bragg and board the 5:30 p.m. Skunk for a return trip to Willits. The Skunk will arrive in Willits around 7:30. You can have either an early dinner at Fort Bragg or a late dinner when you get back to Willits.

Ride the Foothills Around Folsom Lake

Approx. mileage: 40

Rating: A

Terrain: Mostly rolling foothills, with some steep grades on either side of the American River and just south of Cool.

Best times for touring: All of the California foothill country is at its best in spring and fall when temperatures are mild. Summer daytime heat can wilt cyclists who aren't used to it, and cold winter days are too harsh for comfortable travel on two wheels.

Folsom Lake Recreation Area is California's most popular state park, and it is crowded with fishermen, water skiers and sun lovers throughout the warm weather months. Cyclists like this part of the country, too, particularly in the spring when the hills are green and the summer hordes of recreational vehicles have not yet arrived.

This loop takes you all the way around the lake, but does not stay close to the water for the most part. There are many access roads, however, where you can turn off the main roads and ride down to the edge of the water.

Folsom makes a good starting point. An older part of town has been rebuilt into a quaint shopping area with antique shops, high sidewalks, wooden overhangs, and the falsefront stores that were characteristic of construction in the 1860's. Included in the array of shops is an excellent store for Indian crafts, an ice cream parlor and a couple of restaurants.

If you plan to spend more than one day in this area, consider an evening at the Gaslight Theater, where old time melodramas are enacted on weekends. North of town is the Folsom City Park Zoo. It's not too large, but has enough animals to entertain you during an extra hour or two between rides.

There are a number of other points worth visiting around Folsom. The dam is open daily, and you can take an hour-long tour down into the powerhouse.

An older powerhouse, this one built in the 1890's to generate electricity, is on the river near Folsom and can be visited on weekends.

If you have younger folks in your bike touring party, don't overlook the Natoma Fish Hatchery at the southern tip of Lake Natoma. It's open daily, and children especially like to look at the millions of salmon and steelhead fingerlings.

On your ride up to Cool, watch for the construction sites for Auburn Lake Dam and the new highway bridge. The toughest part of the ride is right here —the grade into Cool, the dip in and out of the river ravine, and the climb into Auburn.

Cool and Auburn are famous names in the gold rush history of California, and Auburn has a popular Old Town with some original structures and many that have been refurbished into office buildings. The Placer

County courthouse sits in the square that was used for hangings back in rowdier times.

The run from Auburn back into Folsom has some hills, but nothing like the Cool-Auburn area. Traffic can be heavy in here, though, and the blind curves and hills add an extra element of danger.

Granite Bay is the most popular camping area with cyclists. There is a beach and boat launching ramp so it also draws a big crowd of water skiers and fishermen. Other campgrounds include Beals Point and Peninsula; but during summer, it's often hard to find a space at any of these very popular sites.

Picnicking is simpler; try the shaded areas at Beals Point, Granite Bay or Dyke 8.

Don't be surprised if you're passed on the road by cyclists in a hurry. This is a favorite training ground for the racers in the Sacramento area, and some of them even take the 40-mile spin around the lake in the evenings after work.

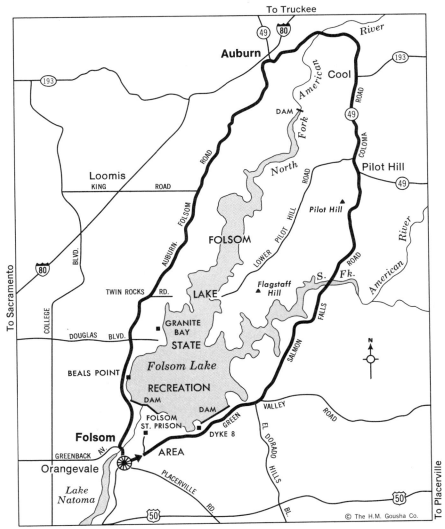

Monterey to Carmel Via 17-Mile Drive

Approx. mileage: 30

Rating: C

Terrain: Flat or gently rolling.

Best times for touring: Good throughout the year—but only on weekdays. Because of traffic congestion, the Seventeen Mile Drive is closed to bicyclists on all weekends and holidays, and during special events such as the Bing Crosby Golf Tournament. To avoid disappointment, it's wisest to write or call in advance to make sure the Drive will be open on the day of your choice. (Del Monte Properties, Pebble Beach, Ca. 93953. Tel. (408) 624-6411.)

The rockbound coasts of Pacific Grove, the forests and homes along the Seventeen Mile Drive, and the quaint shops and atmosphere of Carmel highlight this tour of the Monterey Peninsula. You can start at either end; in Monterey, the intersection of David Street and Lighthouse Avenue is a good starter.

From there, take David Street toward the bay and then turn left onto Ocean View Boulevard, which follows the coastline through Pacific Grove. The entire coastal area along Ocean View Avenue is designated as Pacific Grove Marine Gardens Park.

As you approach Lovers Point, you're likely to see skin divers practicing their skills in the cove. Beyond Lovers Point, the road is flanked by a beautifully landscaped garden all along the ocean to Asilomar Avenue.

The scenery is quite spectacular here, with panoramic views of the ocean surf pounding against sculptured rock, sand dunes covered with ice plant, and the dense groves of trees in the background. At low tide, there are many tide pools worth exploring (but do not take anything from these areas). At the southern end of Sunset Drive you pass by the Asilomar Conference Grounds; from here, there is a very fine view along Moss Beach to the south.

Seventeen Mile Drive (free to bicyclists) offers more spectacular views, plus cypress—forested slopes, famous golf courses, elegant homes and the rugged coastline. Small herds of deer are commonly seen grazing near the Monterey Peninsula Country Club. Take the short spur roads to Bird and Seal Rocks for the always entertaining performances of the area's natural denizens.

South of Seal Rock is Fan Shell Beach, one of the most beautiful on the entire ride. After you pass through the Cypress Point Golf Course, you enter a grove of Monterey cypress. The famous Lone Cypress is a good stopping point if you're in need of a rest.

Plan on spending a few extra minutes enjoying the views from Pescadero Point. Below you is the Pebble Beach Golf Course, Carmel, and Carmel Beach City Park, with the waters of the bay shimmering in the background. Beyond are Carmel River State Beach and Point Lobos State Reserve.

From this point, there is a steep downhill run out of the Del Monte Properties and into Carmel. Ocean Avenue is the heart of the downtown area; it's a stiff climb into town, and you'll probably wind up walking most of the way. And walking can be very pleasant, since it affords you plenty of time to look in store windows and watch the tourists on parade. At the top of the business district is a park at the corner of Ocean and Junipero Avenue; this makes an excellent stop for lunch, especially because the Mediterranean Market across the street provides a wide selection of food and drink.

On your return to Pacific Grove, make the last part of the trip via Asilomar Avenue and Lighthouse Avenue. Point Pinos Light Station is open on Saturdays, Sundays and holidays from 2 to 4 p.m.

On Lighthouse Avenue, you pass the Butterfly Trees, where the Monarchs spend every winter. The butterflies can best be seen on clear days from October to March.

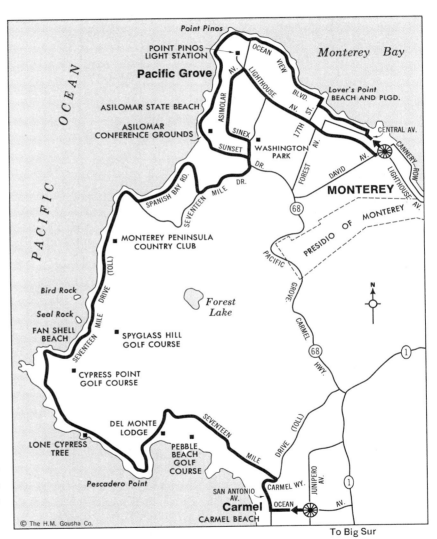

Riding the Rim of Lake Tahoe

Approx. mileage: 70—lake loop. 32—south loop.

Rating: A—lake loop
B—south loop

Terrain: Hilly with several stretches of flatland. Altitude reaches the 6,000 foot level.

Best times for touring: Late spring and early fall are best. Hordes of tourists flock to the lake in the summer between Memorial Day and Labor Day. In winter the deep snows are against you.

Everything complimentary written by Mark Twain and a long succession of admirers is still true about Lake Tahoe. It is just becoming harder to see the lake for the crowds of casinos and condominiums that are spurting up along the shore and back woods. But, even through all the real estate developers' flags and banners ordering you to come and buy, long glimpses of beautiful Tahoe break through. Now is the time to make this trip.

If you must cycle during the summer try to avoid the weekends. Because there are some steep hills and the altitude is high (use low gears and check your brakes), you may want to make a camping trip of it. Campgrounds ring the lake. Be prepared for chilly nights. (If you need to rent bikes, Mike's Bike Rentals is open from Memorial Day to Labor Day at the corner of U.S. 50 and Fremont Street in Bijou.)

Start at South Lake Tahoe and strike out along its wide, congested main street, U.S. 50, for Stateline. Once in Nevada you will pass a city of casinos and clubs and soon climb up the east section of the Rim of the Lake Drive. Past beautiful Zepher Cove, you tunnel through the mountainside and continue on U.S. 50 inland a bit until you turn onto State 28.

Along with the big ski complex and housing development at Incline Village is Ponderosa Ranch, the "Bonanza" home of the Cartwrights of TV fame.

The ranch, open daily from 9 a.m. to 5 p.m., has exhibits, horseback riding, and an evening barbecue; admission.

Circle Crystal Bay from high above and drop down by Kings Beach for a length of fairly flat terrain. The north end of the lake is the last to be developed so you will notice some change in architecture as you pedal toward the western shore. Some of the newer mountain architecture is innovative, contrasting with the traditional homes.

The vistas along the California side past Meeks Bay and Emerald Bay are spectacular and famous, moving Mark Twain to write, "As it lay there with the shadows of the mountains brilliantly photographed upon its surface, I thought it surely must be the fairest picture the whole earth affords."

A few miles past Emerald Bay is the Lake Tahoe Visitor Center, worth a stop for information about the entire area. There is a 30-foot chamber that allows you to observe various types of trout and salmon.

If you feel like an added leg on your Tahoe tour, now is the time to take off on the south loop. Fallen Leaf Road is a narrow, winding lane that takes you through fir and pine forests and past green meadows. There is a climb up Tahoe Mountain Road over the crest of Angora Ridge and into some of the area's undernourished real estate developments.

Ride on Lake Tahoe Boulevard to upper Truckee Road where you have views of the forested Tahoe Basin. Stay on this road, cross State Route 50, and continue along the narrowing valley. You will see the ranch house and slaughterhouse of the pioneer Celio Ranch and remnants of rustic cabins.

A good lunch stop with water and restrooms is available at Alpine Campground before you make the climb to State 89 and the long downhill run to U.S. 50 and Pioneer Trail.

Pioneer Trail is just that. The road that once led wagons now guides you through the green forest back to South Lake Tahoe's suburban sprawl.

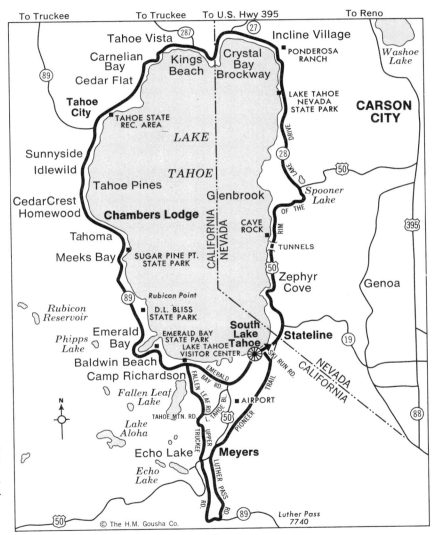

131

Along the Ocean to Sunny Santa Barbara

Approx. mileage: 28

Rating: C

Terrain: Mostly flat with a few grades. Rural roads parallel freeway along the Pacific.

Best times for touring: An excellent ride, any time of year.

Perpetuating mission architecture and early California history, Santa Barbara is the destination of this oceanside tour. From the beach community of Carpinteria to Santa Barbara, spreading from a gently curving beach back to the rugged Santa Ynez Mountains, the round trip is an easy 28 miles along lightly traveled roads that run parallel to U.S. 101.

In Carpinteria, starting at Linden, follow Carpinteria Avenue to Aliso School, turning right to soon cross over U.S. 101. Via Real North is the road you will travel, passing the Santa Barbara Polo Club. You may be lucky enough to see a game in progress—certainly worth a few minutes pause. You will also see a curious Santa Claus after a few miles.

Entering Santa Barbara from the east is a pleasure. Montecito, with its elegant homes set in a landscape thick with trees, is a cyclist's delight. Turn right off Coast Village Road on Hermosilla Drive, then left on Hot Springs Road to Old Coast Highway. You pass Montecito Country Club on the right, tennis courts on the left and soon enter the main section of the city of Santa Barbara.

Take Salinas Street to Carpinteria Street where you turn left. Then right on Milpas, left on Gutierrez and right on State Street, the heart of the city.

Downtown Santa Barbara is a museum in itself with preserved adobes, Presidio Real, El Paseo pedestrian arcade. True to early tradition, the Spanish architecture is echoed in the arched and towered court house and Museum of Art, open daily except Monday from 11 a.m. to 5 p.m.

A complete walking (or cycling) tour of Pueblo Viejo (Old Town) and information on other historical sights is available from the Chamber of Commerce located at 1301 Santa Barbara Street.

Eat lunch in one of the many excellent spots downtown. There are outdoor cafes in the vicinity of El Paseo, where you can window shop for antiques, crafts and books. If time permits, take an extra half hour and casually ride around Santa Barbara.

Just a few blocks from the route at 115 De La Guerra is Hazard's Bike Shop, a stronghold for cyclists since 1914. It is one of the best stocked shops in the West and is capable of making any repairs.

After lunch and sightseeing the route leads out to the coast. Follow Carrillo to San Andres Street (crossing under the freeway), jog right at Canon Perdido to Loma Alta Drive. Continue on Cliff Drive and Castillo to Cabrillo Blvd. On the palm-lined waterfront route you will pass postcard views—with grassy parks, sailboats, artists and swimmers.

The Undersea Gardens near Stearns Wharf is a gateway to

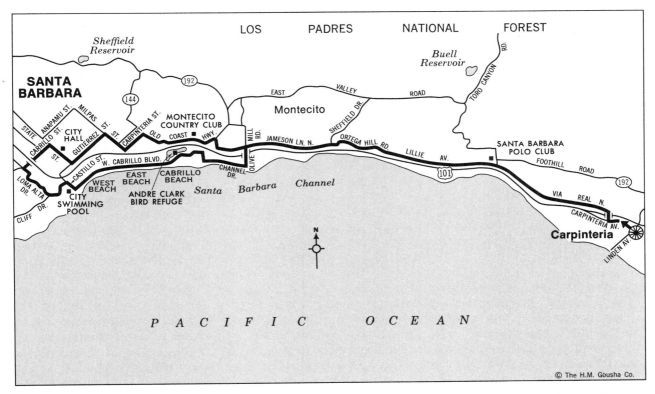

the underwater world. From below the surface you can watch the deep sea creatures and know what you are seeing from the narration of the guide.

Past restaurants, gift shops and periodic art exhibits in the East Beach section of the waterfront follow the well marked bike path along the Andre Clark Bird Refuge. There are spots where you can feed the tame birds and observe the geese, swans, ducks and other waterfowl in this landscaped preserve.

Beyond the refuge a ride down Channel Drive shows you the fabled Santa Barbara Biltmore with its lovely gardens, and the exclusive homes of the Montecito district. Pick up Olive Mill Road and cross over the U.S. 101 freeway. Retrace your route back to Carpinteria.

Danish Pastry, Thousands of Flowers

Approx. mileage: 50

Rating: A

Terrain: Rolling hills in the Santa Ynez Mountains and flatlands along the river. For the most part, traffic is very light along the route.

Best times for touring: An excellent ride any time of year, except on intensely hot midsummer days. Prime tour time is late spring and early summer when the flower fields are in full bloom.

A breathtaking, unique ride, this is one of those tours that really is best seen from a bike. When you are surrounded with several thousand acres of wildly blooming flowers, a car simply whizzes you through too fast.

You need a bike to slow you down long enough to enjoy.

Solvang, a Danish community established in 1911, is a good starting point. Its somewhat commercialized Scandinavian flavor won't really make you think you are in Copenhagen, but it has scores of clean, starched bakeries where you can pick up excellent Danish pastry.

Now hit the road. The ride proceeds south along Alisal Road through mildly rolling land with shady areas past Alisal Golf Course and the rodeo field to Nojoqui Falls County Park. (If you are a bike camper, you may want to camp overnight and begin the tour from here.) The park is a fine location for a rest stop and a hike up to the falls is a pleasant break.

Soon after leaving the park you come to Old County Highway. Make a left on this road which will take you to U.S. 101. You have a short taste of the highway through the Nojoqui Pass before you turn right on Cabrillo Highway (State 1). You'll find some hills in this country as the route winds toward Lompoc. But keep in mind that 200 years ago others were traveling this road by *foot*. So, just shift down, enjoy the rugged scenery and keep pedaling.

Lunch stop is at Lompoc, which has several good cafes. It is off the main U.S. 101 track so there are few tourists. A few miles to the north of Lompoc is the nationally famous site of many missile launchings from the Vandenberg Air Force Base. The superbly reconstructed La Purisima Mission is four miles northeast of town. One of the largest of the original mission chain, it has lovely gardens.

Thousands of acres of flowers—the real thrill of this tour—blossom along Santa Rosa Road. These are commercial fields that produce flower seeds. The fields

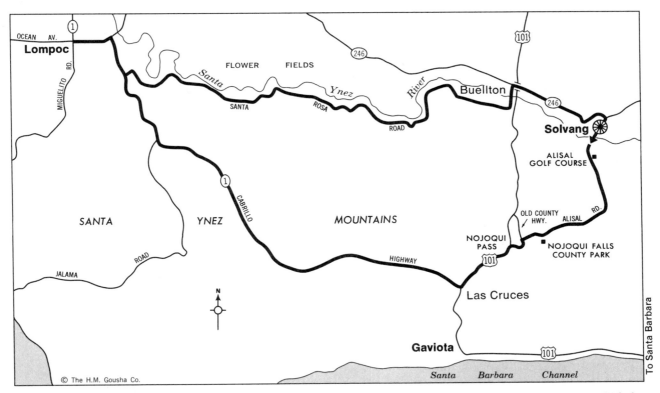

are usually laid out according to color. You will feel as if you are riding through a spacious Mondrian painting—along an area of blue, to fields of blazing orange, on to yellow. This is an incompa- rable sight, providing fantastic bicycling. (If you ever fly over this area—remember to look down over this spectacle.)

From the commercial flower seed fields to split pea soup— the Santa Rosa Road traces the Santa Ynez River and takes you in to Buellton, home of Ander- son's and its famed soup. This is a pleasant stop, for a full meal or just a soup snack.

Cross over the freeway on State 246. From there it is an easy ride back into Solvang.

Solvang to Los Olivos Loop

Approx. mileage: 40

Rating: B

Terrain: Moderate hill climbs and flat canyon roads.

Best times for touring: Good all year but best in spring when wildflowers are blooming.

A word of warning starts this tour—don't settle down at a table in one of Solvang's excellent restaurants before you start. You might decide suddenly to scrap the tour and spend the day just eating your way around town. Instead, save the treat for your return. Get on your bike and leave Solvang via Ballard Canyon Road.

Ballard Canyon is an opening to the rolling ranch country. It becomes Foxen Canyon Road after you cross State 154. The ranchland views are superb. From Foxen the rider swings left onto Alisos Canyon Road for a little exercise over some moderate grades.

Then down to U.S. 101. The well-paved shoulder is excellent, and six flat miles later you head east on State 154 for a view of wildflowers, if you are cycling in the spring.

Historic Los Olivos is next. Here the old Mattei's Tavern beckons the thirsty traveler and gives you a chance to think about the early day carryings-on in this town. Los Olivos grew up as one of fifty California stops on the famed Butterfield Stage Line from Tipton, Missouri, to Los Angeles and north to San Francisco. The stages (top speed, 15 miles an hour under good conditions) enjoyed brief, colorful fame just before the Civil War. The line ended abruptly at the war's end with the opening of the railroad which spanned the nation. Mattei's was built in 1886 on the site of the local Butterfield stop.

Ride along the old San Marcos Pass Road (State 154) for a few miles, turning right on the road to Santa Ynez. It is just a short ride back to Solvang.

Just before you return to the starting point you can visit Mission Santa Ynez, built in 1804. Now restored beautifully after decades of ruin, this mission is one of the most attractive in the chain. There is a curio room with such interesting relics as a horse fiddle and a mechanical organ. The museum contains other well-preserved early California relics and is open daily from 9:30 a.m. to 5 p.m.

Now back to Solvang. After you have a taste of pastry or a meal and browse around the shops filled with Scandinavian handcrafts you may decide to spend another day in this unique town, established in 1911 by a Danish teacher and a Danish preacher as a community for, of course, Danes. The Scandinavian architecture, customs, crafts and food of Solvang have made it a pleasant and unusual tourist attraction.

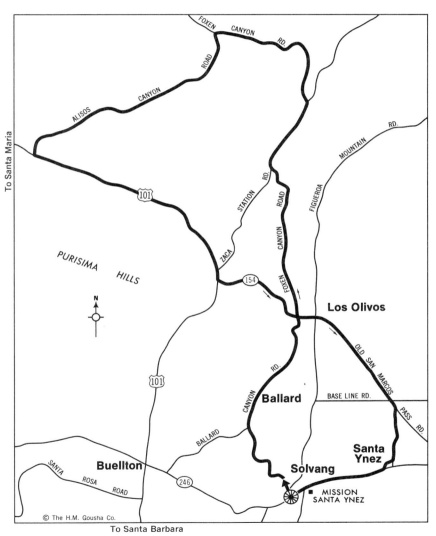

© The H.M. Gousha Co.

To Santa Barbara

See You in Simi

Approx. mileage: 57

Rating: B

Terrain: Some real hills scattered throughout the gently rolling rural citrus country.

Best times for touring: Stay away on the hottest days. A good ride any other time of year.

The improving rider will find this run a good "first" on the moderately difficult scale. The town of Simi in the hill country is the starting spot of the route which takes the rider past citrus groves and rich farmland.

Start at First Street and Los Angeles Avenue in Simi. After half a dozen miles of warm-up past Oak County Park and Moorpark Junior College you enter Moorpark itself. The town has been there for many years, but the building boom is just catching up.

Heading north from Moorpark, the uphill is gradual at first and then, when the route leads to Grimes Canyon, the real hill becomes very apparent. This may be difficult for some but it is short and the grade can be walked.

Once over Grimes, take

Bardsdale Avenue through the town of Bardsdale and pick up South Mountain Road. This rural route takes you to Santa Paula. Sitting in the midst of excellent citrus country, Santa

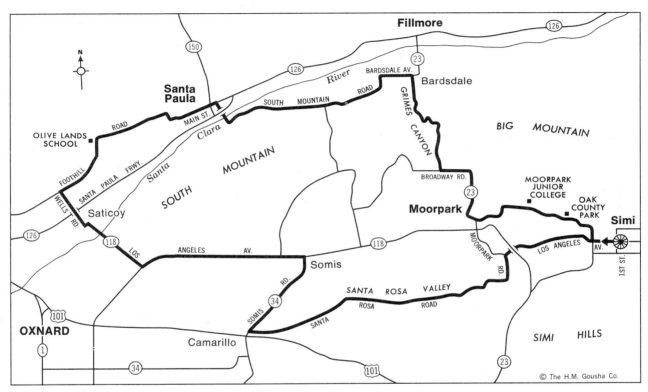

Paula is an interesting ranching town that will provide you with restaurants and snack shops when you want to stop for lunch.

Leave town on Main Street, eventually turning right to Foothill Avenue. Speed on along gently rolling roads, past historical Olive Lands School, and southward through the old town of Saticoy.

Los Angeles Avenue (State 118) shows you more country scenery but you also will begin to notice the invasion of building projects. Somis is the point to turn south along State 34 and follow the railroad tracks to Camarillo. There is more rural travel down Santa Rosa Road; then back to Simi.

San Francisco to Los Angeles—Fog to Smog

Approx. mileage: 480

Rating: A

Terrain: Everything—hilly, flat; straight, winding; narrow and wide roads; windy and calm.

Best times for touring: Anytime except rainy season.

The gem of California bike rides, this should be a must for anyone wanting a week-long bicycle touring thrill. This coast route is neither extremely difficult nor overly easy. It certainly isn't beyond the powers of the average rider with a ten-speed. When possible, prepare yourself ahead of time with local maps. Do not hesitate to ask directions along the route.

Plot your tour and make general plans for each night. On some stretches of the coast trip, motel accommodations are few and far between and even campgrounds are scarce. Good camping places at a reasonable day's ride between are included.

Fill your panniers with a minimum load but be sure to include warm clothing and rainwear for protection against fog and rain. Take along a good lightweight sleeping bag, repair kit, stove (such as Primus) and mess kit, and personal needs.

San Francisco International Airport is the starting place—a good choice, especially if you have flown in with your bike.

Follow these roads across the backbone of the San Francisco Peninsula to the coast: San Bruno Avenue to El Camino Real (State 82), where you turn left. Right on Trousdale Drive and left on Skyline (just before the freeway, Interstate 280). Right on Hayne and left again on Skyline up the hill to the intersection of State Highways 35 and 92.

Cruise down the hill to the ocean at Half Moon Bay on State 92 and turn left down State 1 to begin the first coastal part of the tour. There are several beach parks along this beautiful stretch.

Santa Cruz is a combination resort and university town. There are many bike riders if you need guidance. Take Water Street (which becomes Soquel) left on Gross and left on 41st.

New Brighton State Beach is a good place to camp (the only legal camping place in the area and the last good spot before Big Sur). Reach there from 41st, turning right on Soquel Avenue. About a mile down the road is New Brighton.

The tour continues on Soquel to a right on Freedom; then a left on Bonita (San Andreas Road) to the end. Take a left on Beach into Watsonville and a right on Lee onto State 129. Next go right on G12 to Salinas Road and continue on State 1 to Castroville, the artichoke capitol of the world.

Ride Preston Road in Castroville and out again to State 1, which takes you past Fort Ord. (You may detour through the army post if the freeway becomes posted against bikes.) Past Seaside turn right on Del Monte and cruise into Monterey, famous for early California history and its waterfront.

SAN FRANCISCO-MONTEREY

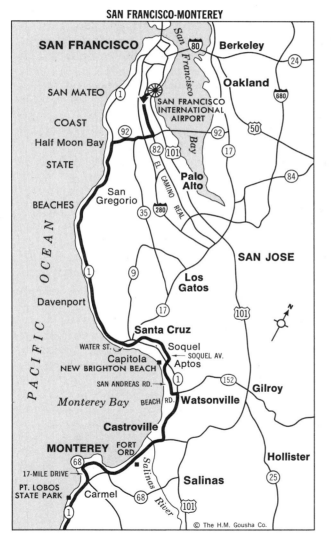

MONTEREY-MORRO BAY

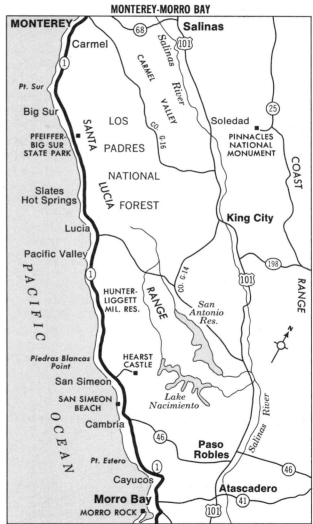

© The H.M. Gousha Co.

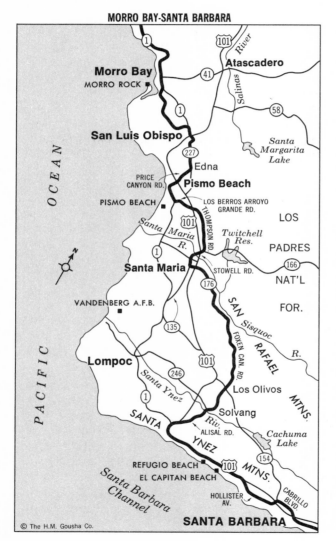

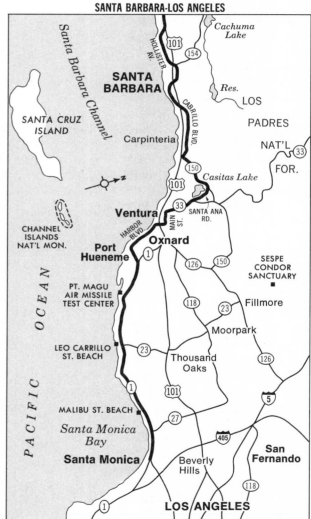

For a side trip to Fisherman's Wharf take a right on Washington off Del Monte, left after crossing some railroad tracks and continue straight through a "Do Not Enter" sign (walk your bike); then go into the parking lot and ride to the other side. You are now back on the route.

To get to the beautiful 17 Mile Drive leave the Monterey wharf area on Pacific, keeping to the right on streets as close as possible to the water. You pass through Cannery Row, erstwhile haunt of John Steinbeck and huge sardine catches, now a tourist attraction. Follow the coastline around pretty Pacific Grove, past the white sands of Asilomar and up Sunset to the entrance to 17 Mile Drive.

(A caution: bicycling is not allowed on the Drive during weekends. In this case, at the entrance, continue up and over the hill to Carmel.)

Leave 17 Mile Drive on Carmel Way, which goes into the village. After exploring the shops on Ocean Avenue, take Junipero Avenue into Rio Drive and turn right on State 1.

This next stretch is one of cycling's most rewarding journeys—the unparalleled coast route to Morro Bay. The road is quite mountainous once you leave Monterey County and the ocean vistas are spectacular. The entire rugged stretch has only spots of habitation but the traffic is considerable. About 25 miles out of Carmel is the famed Big Sur country. Pfeiffer Big Sur has campgrounds.

About 70 miles down the coast you suddenly come upon San Simeon. High above in the hills is the fantastic Hearst Castle. This state monument is well worth a visit for those with the time (tour takes several hours) to see the newspaper mogul's treasures. A warning: locked bicycles are not guarded.

About six miles past San Simeon is a beach of the same name. After the steep climbs along the coast, the campsites here offer welcome relief for tired legs.

When you get to Cayucos, avoid the freeway by taking Ocean to the end where you can get back on State 1.

The next time you get off State 1 is in Morro Bay. The following route can be confusing so inquire locally, if you need help. Take the Atascadero Route 41 exit and cycle under the freeway. Go right on Main, and left as you enter Morro State Park. The road is part of a golf course but it does the job. When you get to a fork in the road, veer right until it dead ends.

Follow this route into San Luis Obispo: Make a left on South Bay Road, right on Quintana, and right on State 1 into town. Cross U.S. 101 and go right on Palm, left on Chorro, right on Pacific and left on Broad (227) down to Pismo Beach. Take the Pismo Beach turnoff to a left on Dolliver and on to State 1, which you follow through Grover City.

Just outside Grover City is the Pismo Beach State Park. If you're camping it would be wise to bed down here. The route goes inland from here and the next campsite is about 50 miles away.

The tour continues along Highway 1 through Oceano. Make a left at the second highway you come to—Cabrillo

Highway—go 4/10ths of a mile and turn right on the road that goes through the small town of Los Berros.

Rolling ranchlands present a change in terrain. Continuing straight ahead, crossing over U.S. 101, follow this back road (it becomes Thompson Avenue) all the way to Santa Maria. Head south of town on Broadway and turn left on Stowell Road (State 176). Follow it into Sisquoc. Out of Sisquoc turn left to Foxen Canyon Road.

Fifteen miles out you come to a fork in the road. Go left to State 154, and left again following the road to Grand. A right on Grand will take you into Los Olivos, the home of the famous Mattei's Tavern.

Refreshments and a rest—then strike out again. Ride right on Alamo Pintado Road and follow it to the end. From here turn right on State 246 into the quaint Danish community of Solvang.

From Solvang, go south on Alisal Canyon Road, past the ranch, to Nojoqui Falls County Park. Turn left on the next road, Old Coast Highway, and follow it to State 101.

About ten miles down 101 you come to El Capitan State Beach. This quiet cove is the theater for some of the most spectacular sunsets on the coast. There are campsites here and it's a nice place to spend a peaceful night.

After Refugio Beach, State 101 turns into a freeway. It is not posted against bicycles, though, so you can ride on the freeway or take a frontage road. At Goleta, the freeway signs indicate "no bicycles." Take the Hollister offramp and stay on Hollister Avenue, which becomes State Street as you enter Santa Barbara.

Follow State Street through the city to Cabrillo Boulevard and travel along the beach front, past the bird refuge and lake. (Or, follow the tour on page 132.) The roads out of Santa Barbara are picturesque and good riding. Crossing under the freeway, turn right on Coast Village Road. Continue on North Jameson Lane to Shefield Drive and Ortega Hill Road. Go right and Ortega Hill becomes Lillie.

Follow Lillie Avenue alongside the freeway and make a left turn on Carpinteria Road.

Follow Carpinteria Road to the end and turn left on State 150 to avoid a choking freeway situation. You will climb past Casitas Lake, see some views of the ocean below and finally coast down to Ventura.

Follow this route: About five hilly miles down the highway take the first right at Santa Ana Road. Turn left when this road ends at Casitas Vista Road; when Casitas Vista ends, go right at Ventura Road. Then left on Thompson, right on Figueroa, left on Harbor, and left on Channel Islands Road. Follow this road to Saviors, and turn right; then left on Hueneme. Just before you get to the freeway, turn right on the frontage road. Make a left on Las Posas and a right onto the Coast Highway.

From there on you're home free. You've won the battle of those accursed freeways, so relax and enjoy the trip into Santa Monica.